TRACI BILD

GET YOUR *girl* BACK

Beth,
Go you girl!
Traci

TRACI BILD

GET YOUR *girl* BACK

Revisit What's Possible for Your Life

How I reclaimed my deepest passions, said yes to myself, and built a life of infinite riches—how you can too!

TBE Publishing

For information, address TBE, 4805 W. Laurel Street Suite 210, Tampa, FL 33607.

Library of Congress Cataloging-in-Publication Data
Bild, Traci
Get Your Girl Back: revisit what's possible for your life / Traci Bild - first edition
p.cm.

1. Empowerment 2. Self-actualization 3. Life skills I. Title.
Library of Congress Control Number: 2015908715
ISBN 978-0-578-16193-9

PRINTED IN THE UNITED STATES OF AMERICA

Photographs courtesy of the author
Cover design by Studio Max
Author photography by Marissa Moss
Book design by Sue Balcer / JustYourType.biz

Get Your Girl Back may be purchased for educational, business, or promotional use. For information on bulk purchases, please contact TB Enterprises Corporate and Premium Sales Department at 1-855-231-9888 or write traci@gygb.com.

First Edition: August 2015

1 2 3 4 5 6 7 8 9 10

Text for this book was set in Garamond Premier Pro.

To my children, Paris and Noah, my constant reminder to laugh,
have fun, and approach each day with childlike curiosity.

To my husband, David, who believes in me
more than I believe in myself.

Table of Contents

Foreword

When I met Traci I was immediately struck by her enthusiasm. She's one of these women who radiates positive energy. As she started speaking to me about her *Get Your Girl Back* book and campaign, she grew even brighter; she lit up like the constellations. And I understood in a flash what drives her life. Traci has a strong desire to help women. She appreciates where she's come from, the distance she's traveled, and the abundance in her present life. She wants to, as the expression goes, "pay forward" to share the wisdom she's gained along the way. She does this so beautifully in *Get Your Girl Back.*

What I love most about her book is that it's not just memoir and not just self-help. It's a wonderful blend of first person narrative and real how-to guidance. It's absolutely action-oriented. Traci is very clear about what you can do to change your life and be in touch with your authentic well of joy. She offers plenty of step-by-step instructions to help overwhelmed women who have lost their enthusiasm and energy. She shows them how they can reconnect and reclaim it. She helps you zero in on what needs to be done to change and recharge your life. That said, Traci is also a strong believer, as am I, in the power of mindfulness—of living in the present moment—with gratitude. And that's a theme that also runs throughout her book.

Of course, I know how tough all this can be. My own schedule is on overdrive. I'm the mother of a girl who just turned five years old, work on the set of *Orange is the New Black,* help manage our family's bi-coastal life, and along with my husband just founded Broadstreet, a production company aimed at developing positive projects for women. But like Traci, I also make sure to meditate, do yoga, and offer myself to community service work. I work with the Women's Prison Association, the Cancer Support Community, and volunteer for several green initiatives. As Traci says in *Get Your Girl Back*, you also have to give back to the world.

You know you can pretty much do anything you have your heart and mind set on. Bild's book stresses this and it's true. But it's not so easy to do alone. In *Get Your Girl Back* you not only have a cheerleader who can inspire you to do your best and specific exercises to lead you to your own power and bliss—but best of all you have a personal coach to help you pull it all together.

Alysia Reiner
Orange is the New Black

A Note to the Reader

Let's talk about who, exactly, your girl is. The way I see it, she's the part of you that is most alive, most vibrant, most potent. Your girl is:

- spontaneous
- fun
- passionate
- curious
- brave
- determined
- decisive
- free-spirited
- excited about life
- hungry to learn and grow
- uniquely you

Don't know your girl yet? Not to worry. That's what we're going to discover. Here's the only thing you need to know now: The quest to get your girl back is about establishing a new state of mind. You're going to evolve a new mindset, and that's going to determine how you operate your life from here on out.

There's going to be some work involved, but I promise it'll be worth it! There are three stages for crafting your new state of mind. First is the *excavation stage,* when you rediscover the girl from your past who was relentlessly happy, fearless, and passionate about life. Second is the *reality check,* when you take a good hard look at your life right now. Third is the *transformation process,* when you get your girl back, introduce her to the woman you are today, and create a life of clarity, direction and purpose.

This book is based on my own quest to get my girl back. It's the story of how she got lost, and how I found her again. The details of your journey may be very different from mine, but the process is exactly the same. How do I know that? I've talked to thousands of women over the past two decades as a motivational speaker, and I've seen miracles. I am certain that you too will find your way into an entirely new way of living.

I want *Get Your Girl Back* to be the most helpful tool you have. I want you to have ideas and inspiration from my own journey. Women have taught one another for generations. We have shared marital tips, childrearing strategies and relationship insights. Now, the teachings are about leading a life of passion and purpose. I share my story in hopes that opening up my life will bring greater happiness to yours.

Let's begin, shall we?

SECTION I

Reclaim Your Passion

chapter one

REFLECT

DEAR DIARY, *HELP!*

It's morning. The alarm rings. You gently tap the snooze button and stretch your arms above your head. No rush. You have all the time in the world. A satisfied grin spreads across your face. Surging with positivity you grab hold of your mental mantra and roll it like a marble in your mind: *The sky's the limit. My possibilities are endless.* Then you count your numerous blessings: your easy-breezy children give you no reason to worry—*nada;* your partner is absolutely perfect, attentive, and generous; your soaring career still allows you plenty of me-time to take care of your mind, body and spirit with meditation, vacations, gym, yoga sessions, mani-pedis and massages. Plus, you enjoy plenty of juicy sex as well as ideal health, thanks to your stress-free life. Whatever you desire, you possess. No regrets. Holding onto all this abundance in your conscious mind, you leisurely roll out of bed and check your reflection in the mirror. *Looking good!* Your eyes are bright and a youthful, boundless spirit is gazing back at you.

Okay. Now *stop dreaming!*

THE REAL WORLD

Chances are if you're like most women with whom I've been in contact—and that's at least 100,000 of us—you're probably feeling a lot more pressure than pleasure these days. That isn't to say you're not experiencing a full, rich life. Whether you're a daughter, sister, wife, mother or grandmother, life moves along and offers myriad experiences. You laugh, cry, grieve and experience moments of wonder. You pour your heart and soul into creating relationships that are deep and meaningful, and work tirelessly to demonstrate your love. Why? Because you're a woman and it's in our DNA to love and be loved, to care, nurture and protect our families. But here's the rub: when we always put those we love and care about first, we end up neglecting our hopeful, carefree, ecstatic and abundantly joyful *selves.* We end up leaving our former optimistic full-of-life girl in the dust. We ignore our birthright of authentic joy.

By any economic or social indicator, the last 35 years should have bumped up the bliss for women. Birth control has given us the ability to control reproduction; we're obtaining far more education and making inroads in many professions that were traditionally male-dominated. The gender wage gap has declined substantially and we're living longer than ever. Studies even suggest that men are starting to take on more housework and child-raising responsibilities. Despite these changes, women's happiness is still declining. This is true of working women and stay-at-home moms, married women and those who are single, the highly educated and the less educated. It is worse for women over 30 years old, and women with kids have fared worse than women without kids. It is indisputable that women are crying out for help. We have achieved so much, yet gained so little.

It doesn't have to be that way. But before I go into my personal revelation of absolute happiness and how I learned to reclaim it, I want to be really clear. I firmly believe there's nothing women can't do—despite what's piled on our plates. We're extraordinary. Consider the millions of single mothers who work tirelessly to provide and care for their children, or the women who belong to what's known as the sandwich generation, who are both raising children and caring for their aging parents at the same time; or women with no children who use their lives through their philanthropic and career contributions to make the world a better place. If there is one thing I know about women, it's that we are more alike than we are different. We share a common bond as givers and long to be our best selves.

THE QUEST TO HAVE IT ALL

It turns out that by setting our goals to have it all, we've lost what matters most—our sense of wonder, our ability to laugh, be spontaneous and have fun. In its place are feelings of anxiety, stress and guilt. No wonder women report feeling unhappy. Every day we wake up with an exhausting pressure to have it all when in truth no one even knows what IT is! In broader terms, "it" doesn't even exist. Trying to have it all is fruitless because it's a term that can't be defined. In short, women are setting themselves up for failure.

> While women are making great progress on the career front, 70% believe the concept of success at both home and work is a myth.

PLAGUED BY GUILT

In addition to the unrealistic expectations we place upon ourselves physically, the emotional toll of trying to have it all is crushing. I've found guilt is a tremendous barrier to happiness among women. Yet, we don't like to talk about it. Embarrassed over self-perceived shortcomings or failures, women create an incredibly damaging inner dialogue that plays like a relentless loop in our minds. While not true, if you say something often enough you begin to believe it:

- "I should be working, not on this field trip today!"
- "I should be at the ball game supporting my son, not here at the office again!"
- "I should stay at home with my kids; I'm a horrible mom for putting them in daycare!"
- "I should get a job that pays and help financially support our family; it's my fault we can't seem to get ahead."
- "I'm the only mom never able to volunteer; they must think I'm awful."
- "I did something wrong, that's why I can't have kids. It's my fault."
- "I should call my dad; he probably thinks I don't care."
- "My house is such a mess—my mother-in-law simply won't understand."
- "My husband's going to leave me, when's the last time I've touched him?"
- "I need to work out; I'm so unfit. Why haven't I exercised in a year?"
- "My mom will never forgive me for putting her in a nursing home."

On and on. Guilt is the "gift" that keeps on giving.

Working Mother Research Institute surveyed 3,781 women and found:

- 51 percent of working mothers feel guilty about not spending enough time with their children
- 55 percent of working mothers feel guilt about the untidiness of their house

THE REAL WAKE-UP CALL

Remember the imaginary woman at the start of the chapter? Well, now let's look at how flesh and blood 41-year-old Amanda, a real wife, mother of two and corporate sales rep greets her morning.

It's 5:45 am and the alarm is blaring. No snooze button for Amanda. She bolts out of bed, pours a mug of coffee, showers, dresses, slaps on make-up, wakes the kids, makes breakfast, throws a load of laundry in the washer, feeds the pets, loads the dishwasher, packs lunch boxes, drops the kids at school, commutes in traffic, works eight to nine hours, picks the kids up, moves the clothes from the washer to the dryer, tidies up the house, unloads the dishwasher, serves dinner (often take-out or microwaved) helps with homework, cleans up the kitchen, folds the laundry and puts it away. She checks work emails, gets the kids showered and ready for bed, scans the clock to see it's 9 pm, sweeps the floor, and heads upstairs to go to bed. On the way up she sees her husband, "*Oh hi honey*!" as she rushes by, feeling incredible guilt over being too tired to spend any time with him. Pulling the covers over her body she breathes a sigh of relief, and the day is done. Yet lurking in her mind is the thought of tomorrow, "I didn't send an email to Rick. Did I sign Jack's permission slip? Where did I put his cleats?" Slowly

Amanda dozes off to sleep in what will be the only time her body rests and her mind stops thinking today.

Can you relate to Amanda? While your life and schedule may be different, odds are there are many similarities. It's no wonder women lack authentic, full-throttle joy. We're on autopilot, moving from one task to another and often doing two to three activities at once. We are consistently on heightened alert, ready and willing to do anything asked of us. Yet when it comes to caring for ourselves, it's an entirely different scenario.

> According to some psychologists, there is a basic difference in the way men and women respond to social stress: for men, it's either "fight or flight" while for women it's "tend and befriend."

Most of us refuse to take time for ourselves and if we do it usually comes with an itchy inner conflict. Women simply avoid putting themselves near the top of the list. As a result there's no outlet to release the tension caused by our maddening lives. Just like a water balloon that bursts when filled with too much H_2O, women unintentionally cause their lives to implode. When the load becomes too heavy, our energy drains and our dreams burst.

OUR PHYSICAL HEALTH

Consider your health. This is the only body you'll ever have. Once your health is lost, it's impossible to get it back. So while making time to get a mammogram might seem selfish because you need to be at the office or at the soccer game, shop for groceries or do the laundry, failure to do so may result in your never going to work, cheering on the sidelines again or being able to handle chores. Refusing to build time into already packed schedules is wreaking havoc in women's bodies. With obesity at an all-time high, women are being diagnosed with diabetes and heart disease at an alarming rate. The bottom line is women are risking their lives as a result of not making it onto that very important to do list.

> Stress can play a part in problems such as headaches, high blood pressure, heart problems, diabetes, skin conditions, asthma, arthritis, depression, and anxiety.

OUR MENTAL HEALTH

In addition to our physical health, women are ignoring their mental health. In a constant state of adrenaline, the mind operates in the fight or flight mode most of the waking day. Just as any muscle needs a break, so does the brain. Women are exhausted and they need to make recharging both their bodies and minds a top priority.

In the past, women had hobbies; they played tennis, Mahjong, cards, sewed or gardened. This kind of down time away from the daily norm allowed women to relax, unwind and refuel for the day or week ahead. While you may have a hobby you enjoy, the question is "are you actually doing it?" FYI: thinking about your favorite hobby and experiencing it are two very different things. Further into this book, I'll review time management ideas to ensure you know how to carve out this critical recharge time, something long past due. I'll also dive deeper into the realities of being a woman in the twenty-first century, and trust me, there are many.

A study in the *New England Journal of Medicine* showed that mentally stimulating hobbies such as reading, playing cards, board games and doing crossword puzzles give your memory a boost.

CONSEQUENCES

What are the consequences of the "everyone-and-everything-before-me" type of lifestyle? How long can we sustain this pace? Proof of its negative effects is showing up in the form of obesity, insomnia and depression among women along with many other ramifications which I will address further into this book. Even worse, women continue to add more to an already full plate in search of ever evasive fulfillment. Sadly, rather than talking about these challenges, women resolutely and silently press forward. Ironically, in the pages of social media everything looks picture perfect. This adds pressure to succeed in every area of our lives—and it can be crushing. If we want things to change then we need to start having an honest conversation.

MY HUGE TURN-AROUND

For a period of my life I tried to have it all, until one day I had a life-changing revelation; in that ah-ha moment, I realized I didn't want *it all.* Instead, I wanted to wake up every day and feel passionate about life. I wanted to laugh more often from deep inside my soul. I wanted to experience those powerful cleansing tears that arise from joy. I wanted to have fun, fun and more fun. Rather than taking my kids to the park and returning emails on my smart phone, I wanted to *play* in the park along with them. I wanted to live in the precious now, not in the future or the past. I wanted to be wholly present with the people I loved most, instead of worrying about what I had to accomplish tomorrow or didn't do yesterday. I wanted to savor every delicious moment—in this exquisite moment.

Did I always know this? Hardly. It wasn't until I made an unexpected discovery which shook me to the core that my true life's calling of finding authentic joy was revealed.

OUT OF THE CLOSET

It was the summer of 2011. I was cleaning out my bedroom closet on a steamy Saturday when I came across dozens of love letters I had written decades ago to my future, and now husband, Dave. A sentimental kind of guy, Dave saved all the letters and stashed the bundle in a box, placing it out of the way on a high shelf deep inside a closet in our Florida home. On a whim, I had pulled the box down, and once I discovered the letters, I sat on the floor and started reading them, one by one. Some were typed and others were handwritten. The papers had yellowed, were delicate with age and felt light like lace in my hands. The letters began when I was twenty and as I read each one over now, 21 years later, I had what I can only suggest felt like an out-of-body experience. Awestruck, I turned from one letter to the next.

"When," I wondered, "was I ever *this* romantic, open-hearted girl?"

I felt a little guilty even asking the question. Shouldn't I just put the letters away, forget it and be satisfied with all I have? Really, shouldn't I be *thrilled* with my present life? After all my marriage is great, my kids, Paris and Noah, are wonderful; I have the business of my dreams, good health, a cushy lifestyle. But no ... I knew there was something missing. A hollowness. What was the difference? What was I missing? As I pored over the letters, I realized it all boiled down to one powerful ingredient: *passion*. As a girl of 20 I was curious about life, hungry to make my mark, and naïve about failure. At 41, I was no longer curious about life, just comfortable in it. I

20-year-old Traci

had pretty much accomplished everything I had set out to do. Yet lurking below the surface was this feeling that an essential element was missing.

I always considered myself a pretty positive person. Yet I couldn't recall ever being as excited about life as I was when I had written these words. It was almost like 20 years later, I was taking a drink from the fountain of youth. As I read the love letters written to Dave, I felt like I was reading letters from his mistress.

Letter after letter detailed our hopes and dreams for the future. But what made these letters even more mind blowing was that *everything* I described—from the coveted beautiful Florida Keys home on the

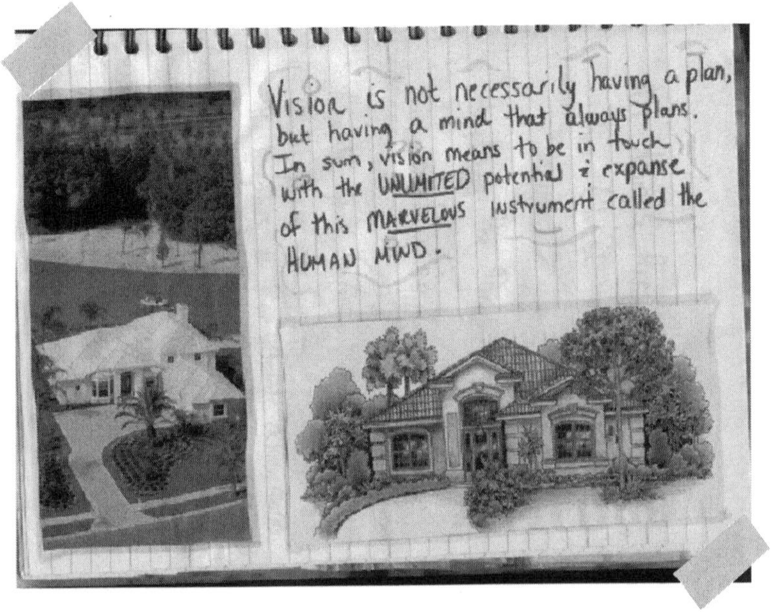

water with lots of space and luscious gardens, to the boat on our dock —we now owned. I wrote about all the places we would visit including Paris, Rome, and London. In those days I'd only seen these cities in movies. We've since traveled to all these locales and way beyond. In another letter I encouraged Dave to hold tight as he pursued the highly difficult field of aviation and his dream of being a captain of a major airline. Now he's accomplished that goal and flies all over the United States.

I was suddenly thrown into the sensation of a reverse déjà vu. I was watching a movie running backwards, unfolding from the end to the beginning rather than the beginning to the end. I knew how the story ended, yet the girl who wrote those letters was clueless. It was like I was standing in front of a mirror as Traci Bild, a woman of 41, looking at Traci Shafer, a girl of 20. In that moment, the past and present collided. It was overwhelming because one woman owed so much to the other. The girl had created the dreams of the woman who was now living them.

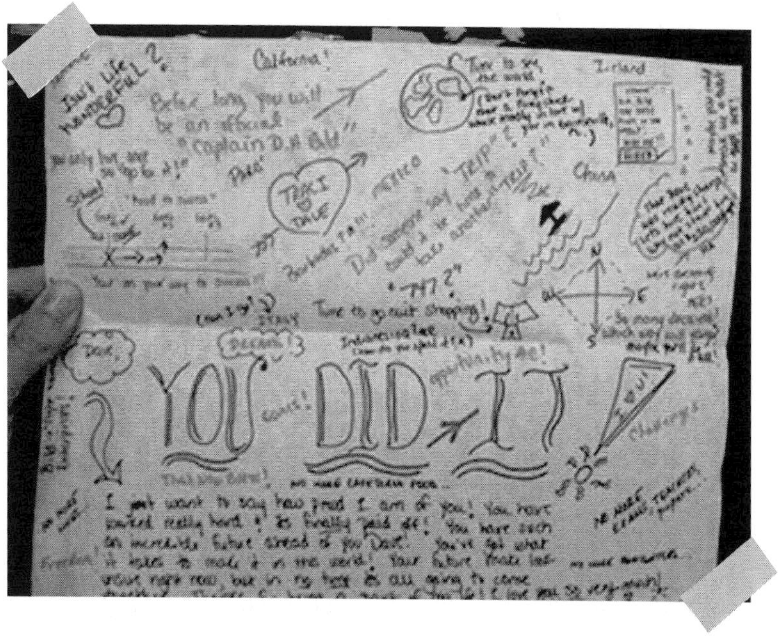

Everything I had written in those letters had come to pass. It was surreal. Each goal and crazy dream had become my reality. It was as if that young girl from the past had had a crystal ball. Wiping tears from my face, I gingerly tucked each delicate letter back into the box and tightly closed the lid.

If you had asked me before that day whether I was the same now as then, I would have said yes, the same but wiser. Sadly though, post-letter reading, I would have to say no. Reading the actual words from 20-year-old Traci brought home a painful message: Time had given me baubles but stolen my raw hunger, drive, and excitement—it stole my deep authentic joy or what I call, my girl.

TAKING IT IN

Getting a glimpse into the girl I once was and feeling the adrenaline, passion, and sheer power of her youth created a thirst for her again. But I decided to keep my newfound realization a secret. I would tell no

How *This* Girl Does It: Yasmine Sharp

I grew up in Santa Fe, California, in a traditional Pakistani family. My dad was incredibly successful in his engineering career. He would tell us, "Excellence will always trump any amount of sexism or racism that you will ever face." We were raised to be independent, highly educated, and whatever you wanted to do, do it, but be really good at it. My mother, while educated, was a stay-at-home mom and played a traditional role. She was up with us at dawn, and made every meal from scratch.

I am the third of four children. There was definitely a double standard between my brothers and my sister and me. There was always an underlying cultural undertone from my dad—"But remember, you're always a woman." This shaped me to be an overachiever. I knew if I kept my nose in a book and made straight A's, I wouldn't upset my dad. It was important to my mom that my sister and me learned to cook traditional Pakistani meals, as well one. I had traveled into the past, grabbed my girl's hand, and brought all that she was into the present. Together my present and past selves would create a future that neither girl could possibly imagine. I was fired up but as it turned out, the journey to discover my girl would require some hard moments of brutal truth. I learned it's not always easy to admit your own shortcomings—yet being honest with yourself is what ultimately allows real and lasting breakthroughs.

In order to move on, I had to confront difficult memories that played a part in the loss of my girl—from watching my big brother become addicted to drugs when I was eleven, to visiting my fragile mother in mental hospitals and battered women shelters, to having to live with friends all through high school. These painful memories of the long-ago past had a bigger hold on my adult life than I realized. Who would have ever thought that a girl who grew up in poverty from a small farm town in Ohio, would own several companies, travel the world, and positively affect millions of lives?

as American food. We spent our summers in the kitchen, while my brothers played outside, so when we girls got married we could cook for our husbands.

Growing into adulthood I knew that I wanted more and learned to contain my fears. In striving for excellence I realized I could conquer both sexism and racism quickly. I learned that it's okay to make mistakes because that's where the greatest lessons are learned. Lastly, that by acting the part for the next job I wanted, if by chance I fell short, I would still be ahead of my peers and ready for that promotion. These three personal rules work well for me to this day.

There is a very real fear in me everyday, but it's part of what drives me. Sometimes I'll tell myself, "Don't let fear of failure manifest itself. Let it drive the will to win.

There's a huge difference between fear of failure and the will to win."

TIME FOR REFLECTION AND CHANGE

I also had to confront the unrealistic expectations I had for myself and reprioritize my life. I took a bold stance and redefined the term "have IT all" into "have YOUR all." The term "have it all" is a farce—no one knows what IT is anyway. I spent a good amount of my adult life chasing something that wasn't definable and no matter how hard I worked or sacrificed, I wasn't ever going to achieve that goal.

Revisiting the facts about my past along with the realities of my present, I began to better understand myself as a woman. These experiences, while difficult, were not crutches, but wings offering the lift needed for my life to take flight. The past is what provided the drive that fueled my life as an adult, and I wouldn't trade it for anything. Having expectations, although unrealistic, ultimately led me to want more for my life and resulted in the creation of the *Get Your Girl Back* movement and the book you are holding in your hands right now.

Reflection provides clarity, acceptance and freedom to move forward into the future in a more enlightened way. These revelations also provided the energy to do things differently or to attempt things far outside my comfort zone. Accepting these challenges gave me moments of exhilaration that are almost indescribable and personal growth that still, to this day, takes my breath away. In this way, one courageous task at a time, the woman I am today reconnected with her girl self and began to lighten up and rediscover the delights of her youthful spirit. I yearned for this girl to show herself again and viewing my past as well as the present through a different lens made that possible.

WHAT ELSE?

Reflecting on my letters sparked ideas for contemplation and personal change. For starters, I had to lighten up, laugh more, think bigger, and leave fear of failure by the side of the road. This new attitude would have to pervade all areas of my life. I made a commitment that I would live every day as if it were my last. Whether I lived to 50 or 90, I was going to squeeze every wonderful moment out of every day of my life. To do that, I had to get to know myself again. I had to regain the girl of the past, who was fearless, fun and romantic. I'd bring her to life again and have her engage with the woman of the present who was cautious, serious and oh-so-wise. They both brought something to the table and I decided to pull the best qualities from each and start anew. Making this decision was profound because it transformed my thoughts, my actions and my life.

The following exercises helped me to find and nurture my girl—and I know they can do the same for you.

GYGB EXERCISES

Throughout the pages of *Get Your Girl Back* and on my website at www.GYGB.com, I challenge you to work through your self-discovery with the same exercises that helped me find my authentic bliss. Along the way, I will ask you to face truths, and take on challenges. Don't worry. You can proceed at your own pace, and your journey is safe in the pages of this book. Your personal, interactive diary will be your unique GYGB guide.

While you may face many similar challenges I share in GYGB, from trying to have it all, to the inability to get yourself on the list, to declined physical and mental health, the good news is you can change direction and revamp your life, starting today. The fact that you are reading this book shows you are hungry for change in your life. Your girl is going to lead the way. I want this to be a fun, passion-fueled process that empowers you to take control of your life, where it's not about having it all but about your all, where priorities are in order, they are honored and when you lay your head on the pillow at night, you experience pure bliss.

Those incredibly personal love letters were like a diary of my younger self. As you move through the pages of *Get Your Girl Back,*

I invite you to consider it *your* personal diary. There's plenty of room for you to write and explore, record memories, brainstorm ideas, work through your feelings, reflect on your life, ponder goals, contemplate dreams, and create specific action steps that will empower you to get your girl back. You can also download our *Get Your Girl Back Dream Journal* which will allow you to create journal entries on the go, as well as attach photos, whenever inspiration snags you.

BEGIN NOW!

COMMIT

Here's your first project. Consider it a dare. I dare you to commit to a changed life. But here's the caveat: If you accept my dare it means that you agree to do the work necessary to bring real and lasting change. Remember your girl? She wasn't on a mission to have it all, she put herself on the list every day and most importantly—she was happy! It's time to get her back.

DEAR DIARY,

I have decided to do whatever's necessary to get my girl back. I am ready to reclaim my deepest passions and build a life of infinite riches.

Signature: ______________________ Date: ___________

Excellent! You are well on your way! Commitment is so important, not just when you're excited about learning a new way to live, but during those times when you might get just a teeny, tiny bit discouraged. (It happens.) When those times come, pop back to this page and remember that you made a vow to yourself—signed, sealed and delivered.

WALK DOWN MEMORY LANE

Imagine you're standing in front of a mirror and seeing not the woman you are now but the girl from your past. I'm talking about the girl who knew what she wanted, who was confident and in control of her life. Nothing could stop her. Think back to a time in your life when you felt passionate, vibrant, and alive.

> THINK LIKE THIS GIRL
>
> *There is a fountain of youth. It is your mind, your talents, the creativity you bring to your life and the lives of people you love. When you learn to tap this source, you will have truly defeated age.*
>
> *—Sophia Loren*

Was there a time when anything was possible and no one could tell you otherwise? You knew deep inside that you were meant for something great? This is the girl I want you to rediscover and bring back to the forefront of your life. It might have been when you were 18 and had just graduated from high school. Free from parents, you were able to make your own decisions and experience what it was like to be an adult. You didn't have responsibilities like debt, children or a relationship to worry about. You were young, free, and the world was yours for the taking.

Maybe it was the time you got off the couch, took control of your health, lost weight and ran a marathon. You felt the power of running through the finish line and succumbed to the rewards of a year of discipline, hard work and pure determination—and knew that nothing would ever be impossible again. There are other ways to remember your girl. Something as simple as a song, a movie clip or a smell can transport you back. Whenever I hear the song, "Let the Good Times Roll" by The Cars, I immediately recall my best friend Michele and me in high school cruising around in her car, "The Turd." It was chocolate brown and the size of a wind-up car but it had wheels and it got us where we needed to go. We would drive for hours, without a plan, and just talk, laugh, and sing to our favorite tunes.

Think back and try to recall the best times in your life. Perhaps it was when you were in college, just married, landed your first real job, got your children out of diapers, or quit a job you hated to find something you would love. It could have been an obscure year with no significant meaning other than you felt great and were happy. You can't explain it and there is no rhyme or reason, you were simply happy.

Here's another way to think back: Make a timeline of the different chapters in your life. If that's too hard, divide the line up by decades, and note the most important thing that was going on for you at that time.

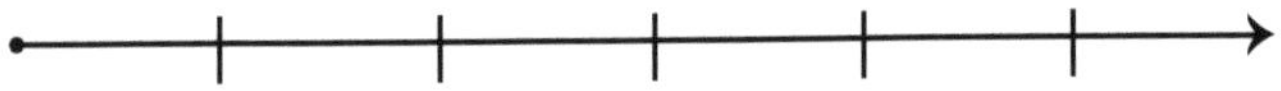

Time Line

Write dates for each event in time order from left to right. Add details along the line.

How *This* Girl Does It: Donna Cutting

When I think of my girl—completely free and exactly myself—it was when I was eight. I used to put on talent shows in the backyard. My friend Lisa and I formed a band, which was really just us singing into our hairbrushes. We called ourselves the "Royalettes." My dad built the stages. I put up flyers everywhere, promising free refreshments (usually popcorn). I remember having such confidence during my performances even when, once, part of my costume came apart. I kept doing my high kicks and thinking, *the show must go on!*

As I got older, insecurity crept in. One year, Sister Paulette picked me to sing "O Holy Night" in the school Christmas play. Afterward, a friend told me, "You don't even sing as well as you *think* you do." That statement left a hard-to-heal wound. In high school, I auditioned for plays but always ended up working on costumes and makeup. I was devastated when I didn't get a part. Once I asked a teacher about upcoming auditions. He told me the time and then added, "But if you don't make it, you're still going to work on costumes, right?" I immediately internalized this message as, "No matter what you do, you're not going to be good enough to make it." I studied theatre in college. I got roles and got on stage, and felt my confidence coming back. I ended up leaving college and going to Seattle to pursue acting, but was so terrified of auditioning that I never went on a single one.

I ended up in a job as an elder-care activities director. I brought my theatrical side into my job, but I felt that it wasn't what I started out to do. I was reminded of this during an art class I took. I was creating a dancer out of clay, but I didn't like how it was coming out, so I changed it to an ashtray. The instructor later told me, "Donna, don't cover up your dancer." It took me years to realize what she was really saying. Taking her cue I ended up dancing right into my dream—as the founder of Red Carpet Customer Service I speak nationally, consult with companies to improve their customer service experience, and published a successful book, *Red Carpet Customer Service* and I'm just getting started!

RETRACE YOUR STEPS

Good job! Now take a deep breath, then go back and circle the ones that truly, really were special. Next, go back and number the first, second and third best moments of your life. This exercise will help you to retrace where you have been so far so you can better direct where you are headed as you move into the future.

If the timeline doesn't stimulate your thoughts, maybe there's a diary, a calendar or a scrapbook you could go back through for inspiration. What were you doing, what did you look like, how did you feel, who were your friends? Were you single, married or recently divorced? Were you young and broke and living with your parents but never happier?

There's no right or wrong here. You want to identify that moment in time when you know you had your girl. For me, what I liked about my girl was that she was fearless and romantic. She had huge dreams that she pursued with a vengeance—and when she failed, she just scraped off the dirt and kept moving forward. I was between 23 and 26. I had just moved into my first apartment in Tampa, FL, was waiting tables (making barely enough money to pay the bills) and had started my new speaking business which I still have today. What I liked the most was her zest for life and the size of her dreams. Those dreams resulted in a company that currently has 25 employees, operates nationally and landed on the *Inc. Magazine's* "Fastest Growing Companies in America" list in 2013.

Okay. Now I want you to write down what your girl was like by finishing this thought:

I felt totally excited about life when I...

____

____

____

Not everyone can find such clear memories. Don't worry! If you feel you never really had your girl, begin to think about who she might be. What traits have you always admired in other women? What have you always wanted to do but never let yourself?

LOOKING AHEAD

Jot down a few of the traits you'd like your girl to have:

____

____

____

____

Uncovering your girl may come to you easily or it may prove to be difficult. It depends on how many walls you've put up over the years. But it is never too late to put everything you've got into finding your girl. Together we are going to get her back!

OFFER YOURSELF A HEART-TO-HEART CHAT

Now I want you to take a few moments to write down what your girl would say to the woman you are today:

____

____

____

____

____

All right! The conversation has begun! As you follow along in *Get Your Girl Back*, your girl will continue speaking to you. But remember that to hear her, you have to really listen. That's why I'm asking you to be open and receptive to the ideas and emotions that come to you as you travel through this book. If you feel like crying, grab a tissue and let it out—don't repress anything. For once you are going to take the time to work *on* your life instead of just living *in* it.

How *This* Girl Does It:: *Lili Kohr*

I grew up in a strict household, a free spirit who wanted to be around people all of the time. I was always breaking rules and getting in trouble. My parents actually put bars on my bedroom windows, but that didn't keep me from sneaking out. My senior year of high school I sold copies of my principal's signature for students to use on passes to get out of school. I was always breaking curfew. I grew up in a dictatorship regime in my country. My uncle, who lived with us, was second in command, and my father was a policeman working for the U.S. government. I grew up surrounded with security like AK-47 rifles as a way of life. I was living in the Republic of Panama during the dictatorship of Noriega.

When I was 17, my parents sent me to college in the U.S. After college, I knew I didn't want to work for anyone. So I decided I might as well sell something, so at night after waiting tables, I would embellish headbands with sequins. I also sold homemade cakes door to door, but none of my attempts made a profit. Until I met my husband.

He helped me re-train my negative thoughts to dreams. For the first time in my life, I had a man who saw the best in me. I went from selling handbags on eBay to opening up six stores. I was successful. We got married and we now have four beautiful children.

As a young woman, I never dreamed because I was never allowed to dream. I was afraid to dream because I was afraid of failure. I'm no longer living in fear. The tiger inside me has been let out of her cage and she's roaring.

THINK LIKE THIS GIRL

If it scares you it might be a good thing to try.

ASK THE BIG QUESTION: WHY DO I WANT TO GET MY GIRL BACK?

Let's dig down a little more to see what could happen if you fight to get your girl back. I've discovered that if I know what I'm fighting for, I'm more likely to succeed and to feel happy and fulfilled while doing so. My company had doubled in size each year for the past four years. Things were going so well that I was even thinking we should slow down our growth and go more into stabilization mode. Yet part of me, that crazy entrepreneur who loves a great challenge, bailed at the thought of sitting back like that. So I spent some time coming up with my "whys." Why exactly did I want to grow? I discovered that for me, growth was less about financial success than about feeding my need for adventure, challenge and a feeling of accomplishment. I'll share my list with you:

WHY I WORK

1. To provide an extraordinary quality of life for my family
2. To feel accomplished
3. To be challenged
4. To grow
5. To have financial security
6. To make a difference
7. To travel
8. To leave a legacy
9. To enjoy small things
10. To be engaged in life's flow

I posted this list on the wall in front of my desk, right at eye level. When making tough decisions, I look at the list and use it as a guide. My answer must be in alignment with my "Why" list. The list means that every day when I wake up and walk into my office, I have evidence of the values behind how I use my time, energy and effort.

Just as I work with greater purpose because I'm now clear on the why behind the work, I would like for you to understand the why behind getting your girl back so that you are able to delve into this book with purpose and passion. Consider the various compartments of your life to include relationships, health, finances, career, home and more. What might a totally passionate, excited, committed-to-life "YOU" bring to those areas?

Go for it! Why do you want your girl back?

____

____

____

____

> THINK LIKE THIS GIRL
>
> *Imagine how it would be to wake up every day excited, alive and passionate about your life. Imagine how it would feel to be healthy and fit, to have energy, and peace of mind. You can do it!*

How's that feel? It's work, I admit. But doesn't it feel deeply rewarding to dig into the wellspring of your life? With effort, you can find the youth of your past and begin to laugh again, be spontaneous, find wonder in the smallest of things, love your career, master your finances, get control of your home, and accomplish literally anything you set your mind to.

I once heard former President George W. Bush say that his presidency was but a chapter in his life. He had a chapter before his presidency, one during and one after. Consider getting your girl back the next chapter in your life. Bonus: You get to write the story! The only way you'll know what's possible for your life is to step up and give it all you've got. I did and I am constantly in awe about the results. I am amazed by the sheer power given to us to do, be and have whatever it is we want in life. I have moved to an entirely new level of living. I wake up every day filled with excitement and gratitude. While others complain, I give thanks. While others groan they have no control over anything in their lives, I exert control over every element of my life. While others complain that life isn't what they thought it would be, I find peace in knowing that life follows the plan I have for it. Life is what I make it. And your life is what you make it!

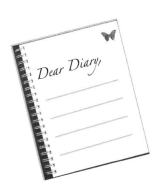

REFLECT LIKE THIS GIRL:
Chapter Summary

1. It's not enough to have a good life. You deserve a *great* life—where you dare to dream and make your dreams come true. Now you have the tools to make it happen. It's hard work, and begins with a written commitment to getting your girl back.

2. Despite many gains, women's overall happiness is declining. We have to fight to take back our joy!

3. Your girl is that part of you that was and is most passionate and alive. She wants to know the woman you are today. Bring your two selves together by spending time finding what excites you, reviewing memories. Think about what traits you admire in other women that you'd like to have for yourself.

4. When you know why you need to do what you need to do, you're stronger and more committed to doing it.

5. You have courage you haven't even seen yet. Believe it!

chapter two

Purge

GET THOSE FEELINGS UP AND OUT!

One of the greatest benefits of living life on your own terms is that you get to choose the exact experiences you want. I just turned 42. I love birthdays. I love aging. With each year I feel more confident, wise and in control of my life. What I *don't* feel in control of is my physical self. No matter how many people told me what to expect, I simply was not prepared to see my body work against me rather than for me. Learning how to cope with the changes in my health has been downright frustrating and one of the most difficult challenges in my adult life. While I used to be able to drop five pounds in a week and eat what I wanted, that is simply no longer the case.

THE BARRIER

What about you? What's challenging you today? Perhaps it's not your body. Maybe it's your finances, a home full of clutter, or a job that sucks the energy right out of you. We all have our battles and for many of us they stem from the past. A woman who is 50 pounds overweight looks in the mirror and sees the girl nicknamed "Pig" by the boys in her high school. The woman buried in clutter grieves over the loss of her mother by saving everything for fear she might need it one day. The woman working a job she hates believes she is lucky to have any job at all because her husband tells her over and over what a piece of trash she is. Big or small, whatever it is that's blocking you from being the girl you want to be, it must be addressed.

In this chapter we will identify some of the mental blocks keeping you from stepping into the life you were meant to live. You will stand up for yourself and take control. On your quest to get your girl back, if your health is an obstacle, you will fight. Meaning, if you need to lose weight, you will do it because your health is worth it. If you need to increase muscle tone and reduce body fat, you will do it. If you need to clear your mind to allow for a good night's sleep, you will do it. If you need to eat less meat and more vegetables, you will do it. You will get in control and create the mind, body, and spirit you want, not the one you now have.

If finances are creating stress in your life, you will stop making excuses. You will establish a savings account, live within your means, cut coupons, find hobbies other than shopping, and see what it's like to have money left over at the end of the month.

If clutter creates anxiety, you will spend 15 minutes a day decluttering an area in your home, one weekend a month, removing items that simply take up space. You'll create new habits to bring order and harmony to your living environment. Whatever the barrier, you will succeed. Remember, you get what you put your focus on. No task is too big.

THINK LIKE THIS GIRL!

Who you were yesterday or even today does not dictate who you will be tomorrow.

FACING REALITY

Just as Michelangelo sculpted the statue of David out of stone, you will work day by day, chapter by chapter to get your girl back. When Michelangelo was asked how he created such magnificent sculptures, he responded, "The sculpture was already there. All I did was remove the stone."

The girl you long to be, the girl you were when you were at your very best, is inside you screaming to get out. Your job is to chip away the stone. To do that, you must address what is holding you back. It's time to excavate those memories that haunt you and prevent you from moving on in life. Whether it's the frustrations in your marriage, anger at your parents, the mounting pile of bills on your desk, or negative self-talk that junks up your mind, I want you to get it out. Then you will let it go.

As a professional speaker and coach for the last 20 years, I have had the honor of working closely with hundreds of thousands of women. I have an incredible amount of respect for women and am constantly amazed by all they do and the many burdens they carry. Only a woman can possibly understand the life of another woman. Think of all a woman accomplishes in the course of one day:

She gets herself and her children up at the crack of dawn for school, feeds the cat, makes breakfast, cleans up, throws a load of laundry in the washer, folds another, puts those clothes away, maybe even irons, gets everyone dressed, packs lunches, gets backpacks organized with papers signed, homework checked, kids dropped off at school, and promptly heads off to work for eight to ten hours.

On her lunch hour she plans the week's meals, stops on the way home to buy groceries, puts them away, makes dinner, cleans up, bathes the kids, assists with homework, throws in another load of laundry, picks up the never-ending clutter, does another load of laundry (because that never ends), tries to sit down to read the paper, to be interrupted three to four times only to give up and go clean some more. She plays with the kids, gets teeth brushed, reads a story, tucks everyone in, and then takes a big deep breath when she realizes that everyone is happily snuggled up in bed. She smiles as she realizes that she has a minute to herself. She walks downstairs and there waits her husband. "Hello honey...."

THINK LIKE THIS GIRL

Given a cape and a mask I am fairly certain I could save the world.

—Unknown

While this is my reality, I imagine it looks a bit like yours. You may not have small children anymore but instead grumpy teenagers who hate you or at least act like they do, or aging parents who have become more like your children and need help on a daily basis. Whatever stage of life we're in, women have a lot on their plates. As a result, many become resentful, angry and confrontational. This is no way to live.

So, right here and now, I want to address the fact that you, as a woman, have more than your fair share of work. It's not fair but it is what it is. Over time women have become responsible for juggling two full time jobs: Our families and our careers. I'll be honest. It's nearly impossible to manage and has resulted in failed marriages, poor health and depression. Girlfriend, you are not alone. I want you to take a moment and just get it out. You are going to write down those things that are weighing on you and that have been stealing your life and the joy you so deserve.

I'll start with my own simple example. I hate the fact that I have to clean all the time. No matter how hard I work, or how much laundry I do, there is always more to do. It drives me nuts that my kids throw their socks and pants on the floor by the laundry basket versus putting them inside the basket that is right there. I wish that for once someone would say "thank you" for all the work I do because I work very hard to create a sacred home environment where my family feels peace, order, and harmony. Hello, is anyone noticing what I do at all or am I a maid? By the way, where does all this crap come from? I hate that after a day of work, it takes me an hour to adjust my brain from being CEO to being mom and wife. Yet instead of understanding that I need to transition, I am told that I am being difficult. Why is it that men get down time after work but women just keep on working? Is this a double standard? I hate that I'm the only one who sees the clutter, the toys on the floor, and the fact that the litter box smells like an outhouse that has sat in the sun for a week. It drives me nuts that no else seems to notice that the trash can is overflowing or that there is mold growing in our refrigerator. I am tired of always feeling rushed. There is literally always something to do. I can't even go to the bathroom without being interrupted or called for. What's with that? I love my family more than anything in the world. Yet at times I am simply exhausted and nothing would mean more than a simple acknowledgment for just one thing that I did for them today.

> THINK LIKE THIS GIRL
>
> *You do not have to be the prisoner of your own life. You can take charge, one task, one thought, one action at a time.*

Your turn. What's pissing you off and keeping you from happiness and fulfillment?

Okay. Now. Take a deep breath, hold it to the count of five, and let it go. When I say let it go, I mean not just your breath but everything that has been eating at you for the last day, week, month or year. Let it flow out of you. Surrender it to the universe. Give it away to the air. Now do that two more times. Enjoy the feeling of release. There. Isn't that better? Don't worry if, in a day or a week, the grudges and resentments come back, or new ones arise. This is a simple exercise you can do any time you need it.

CONFRONTING THE PAST

Now that we have dealt with what's happening right now in your life, I'd like for you to dig back a bit into your past. Most of us have burdens we've carried for years that still rob us of joy and possibility in the here and now. On your quest to get your girl back, I encourage you to address anything and everything holding you prisoner right now. We are going to look your fears, failures and traumas square in the eye and then let them go, forever.

THINK LIKE THIS GIRL

We can't do better until we know better. Stop beating yourself up for what you didn't know.

Earlier this year I had a spontaneous opportunity to look back over my own past. I was conducting a seminar at the beautiful Opryland Gaylord Hotel in Nashville, Tennessee. After my session I decided to take a walk through the hotel. While strolling through the huge lobby, I saw a water fountain giving an amazing show. As tantalizing French music played in the background, the water put on an amazing display of dance, light and intrigue. Rising and falling, swaying and splashing, it called out to me to engage. I decided to sit for a while and work on this book. Yet, as I typed I couldn't take my eyes off the water for fear that it would know I wasn't paying attention. So I typed blindly and watched the show.

I typed and watched—and wondered how I even came to be here. After 20 years of traveling to some of the most amazing hotels in the world and seeing things I never dreamed I'd see, I am still in awe. How did I, Traci Renné Shafer, get here? I've asked myself that question a thousand times. My mom always told me that I could do anything. But a girl like me, from a broken home and a low-income family? A girl like me has very few expectations, and the probability of success is very unlikely.

I grew up in tough circumstances and faced challenges most people in my present life probably wouldn't relate to. When people see me speak, they see a woman with her act together, who is confident and good at what she does. Many assume I went to an Ivy League college and had an idyllic upbringing. Few would believe that I spent my high school years living with various friends because I refused to live in my abusive stepfather's home. No one now would imagine how many days I spent during those years visiting my mother in battered women's shelters and mental hospitals. Like you, I have many painful memories. However, I do not allow them to take up space in my life today. I have left them where they belong—in the past.

Sadly, many people are prisoners to what once was but is no more. Each woman has her own life experience. You may have been abused, molested, abandoned, bullied and told you were worthless—or worse. Some women reading this book have survived things the rest of us could never imagine. As women, from birth through adulthood, we are easy targets. No one comes through childhood unscathed. Rich or poor, black or white, boy or girl, we all have war stories. What's important is that you face up to the past and take a stand. You cannot let yesterday steal your joy today. The past is in the past and that is where it belongs.

THINK LIKE THIS GIRL

It's never too late to have a happy childhood.

THINK LIKE THIS GIRL

If you keep living in the past it will steal your future. Put your focus on what is good now, here today. Give all your energy to the present and to creating the life you are meant to live.

Along the way, many people develop coping mechanisms to help them handle things that come up in life that are unpleasant, including things from the past that they never fully dealt with. My husband, Dave, makes fun of how I deal with unpleasantness. He always says, "You forget the bad and remember the good. How is that?" He's right! I don't know when or how it started but for most of my life I have been able to banish from memory anything bad that has happened to me. The fact is, the past has no purpose or place in my present life. Writing this book has forced me to visit places in time that I have not visited for decades. The coping mechanism I have works for me. What about you? How have you coped with things you'd rather forget? Do you escape into unhealthy habits like eating or drinking too much? Do you beat yourself up every day and destroy your self-esteem? Do you use negative past experiences as an excuse to avoid working toward future success? What do you do exactly?

What is your main coping mechanism?

____

____

____

____

____

In this chapter, I want you to bust free of your prison. It's time to get it out, once and for all, and move on. From this day forward, you will be free of the handcuffs that bind you to the past and keep you from moving freely into the future. This is a time for you and you alone to get it out. As you read and ponder, hold nothing back. I don't care if you end up with tear stains on every page or pages even ripped out. No more nice girl!

Are you nervous? Are you considering just skipping this chapter? It sure would be easier, wouldn't it? I'll be honest. I was a little bit nervous about doing this myself. Even with my coping mechanisms, I felt unsure whether I wanted to "go there." Yet I did. As your girlfriend, let me hold your hand and walk you through to the other side. We are going to dig deeper, look your memories square in the eye, and let the bad ones go.

I realize that many of your memories are sensitive and that there may be things you'd never want anyone else to know. For that reason, don't feel like you have to write anything down. I have provided spaces for you to write should you want to. If you aren't comfortable, simply read the questions and ponder your answers.

THINK LIKE THIS GIRL

Every day you take out the trash and never think twice about all the things you are throwing away. Today, you are clearing out the garbage in your mind. You are going to throw it out and let it go.

But it can be healing to look back—not to get stuck there, but to acknowledge, then say goodbye to those old tales. I'll go first. When I was in high school I was trying to get a job at Dairy Queen. Believe it or not, this was the coolest place to work and only the wealthy, popular kids ended up with the jobs there. Yet my mom had always told me I could do anything so I went for it. I submitted my application and was shocked when my best friend Michele and I were offered the jobs. It was a moment of elation and excitement—we were in! Yet on my first day, my boss Jerry told me that she had called my principal as a reference for me. He told her I was a ditz and would not be a good candidate for the job. As odd as it sounds, I carried this around with me most of my adult life. How could someone I looked up to and trusted think so little of me? I had to remind myself that my new bosses, Jug and Jerry, saw something in me that the principal did not and gave me the job. God had my back because that job changed my life. I learned true work ethic, responsibility, and made amazing friendships. The DQ family became my family.

That wasn't the only time I felt unworthy. No matter how hard I worked, my English teacher never gave me anything above a C grade. I often wondered whether she even read my work. She was more interested in the smart, preppy kids and, although I admired her much more than she knew, she never gave me the time of day. I was invisible to her. She once told me I had horrible writing skills. I wonder what she would think today of the three books I've published? Each time I publish one, I think of her for a moment. As much as I wish her attitude didn't bother me, for years it did.

This feeling of not being good enough stuck with me most of my life. It wasn't until I went in search of my girl that I finally addressed this internal struggle. Prior to my personal journey to get my girl back, I consistently encountered situations where someone told me I wasn't good enough. While at Embry Riddle in college, I worked as an assistant manager for a large retail chain. I went to school during the day, worked as a co-manager of the store at night, and studied after work for as long as I could stay awake. Many times I would work until two or three in the morning due to floor moves, when we rearranged the store. In these situations I would either miss class entirely or show up late. Being in retail I always dressed fashionably.

I was amazed how many people judged me based on how I dressed and thought I was at this school, with a guy to girl ratio of ten to one, simply to land a husband.

One male student came up to me while I was walking to class and said, "You know, I don't know why you're here, you'll never amount to anything. Heck, you'll probably be working for me one day." To this day I can't figure out why or how he could say that to another human being. His words, though short, made a huge impact and made me feel like an imposter. For years I would question myself, "Who am I to think I can do this?" I was putting myself through school, working full time, and the first ever in my family to go to college. As I paid for each semester I had no idea how I would pay for the next, I just kept moving forward taking it one day at a time. The impact of this young man's words lasted for years. Yet after a few tears and with my nose to the grindstone, I moved on. Today, his words have no meaning as I realize they are irrelevant.

> THINK LIKE THIS GIRL
>
> *God has more planned for you than you could ever imagine for yourself.*

According to society, I was not supposed to turn out to be the woman I am today. It just doesn't happen that way. Yet I chose my mother's words over those of my principal, teacher and fellow student. My mother knew me best and influenced my life the most. Is there a person or people who still hold power over you today? Are they just empty memories or are they still handcuffs keeping you prisoner to the past?

As I looked back at these brief yet profound moments in my past, I was forced to ponder the most painful memories. Until the start of this journey to get my girl back, I never realized a common theme of low self-worth that manifested itself in my life. Reflection is critical to healing and to moving forward. Conducting the very exercises that I'll ask you to do in a moment helped me realize for the first time in 30 years that the feelings of not being good enough tied back to my own father. Reliving these stories triggered a theme in my mind and my dad came to the forefront in a big, loud way.

I love my dad and don't blame him for anything. Yet as I dug to uncover my own girl, I realized that having a father, particularly to a woman, is very important. Having a father, yet not knowing him, is even more important. My dad loves me. This I know for sure. Yet most of my life I never saw him. I never knew him until I was in my late thirties. He wasn't a deadbeat dad. He simply lived far away and airline tickets were prohibitive. I only saw him once or twice during the most formative years of my life. I know my dad did the best he knew how to do. He sent cards and Christmas gifts and called from time to time. Yet, looking back, I can see that his absence created emotions of not being good enough for my own father that I would carry around much of my adult life. I did not seek these thoughts out and quite honestly, I never even correlated the effect of being raised without my father to low self-esteem until I began to evaluate my life and "get it all out." Understanding where the feelings of low self-worth came from completely set me free.

> THINK LIKE THIS GIRL
>
> *The truth will set you free.*

BREAKING FREE

Once I understood my past, I used it to positively impact my future. I actively worked to get to know my father and create the relationship I always wanted and deserved. I can tell you that today my dad and I are closer than we have ever been. I still don't see him often, but I make it a point to find him in his RV once a year. I fly to his location and spend the night, talking for hours over cheese and margaritas. For me, this has brought closure and healing. The best part is that the feelings of low self-worth and rejection are gone. The open wound of my past has been healed.

THINK LIKE THIS GIRL

All you have to do is take the first step. Remember, the longest journey begins with a single step.

Where are your wounds? As you ponder your childhood, what is holding you back today as an adult?

____

____

____

____

____

What one person or memory still holds you prisoner?

____

____

____

____

As an adult, was there an incident that stole your confidence, dignity, pride or ability to believe in yourself? What was it?

____

____

____

What do you say to yourself when you look in the mirror? (If you never look, write about that.)

____

____

____

THINK LIKE THIS GIRL

We all do the best we can, with the knowledge we have at the time a situation occurs. You can't do better until you know better. Now you know.

Perhaps it's not someone from the past but instead, something you did that caused you to lose all belief and confidence in yourself. If that's true, what was it?

____

____

____

As children, we failed every day. Learning to ride our bikes, we crashed over and over yet got back up and tried again. I recall in seventh grade failing a geography test three times. I passed on the fourth attempt! Failure is part of the lesson plan for kids. Millions of adults, on the other hand, are paralyzed by failure and let it steal their dreams. Even the sheer thought of facing a flop is enough to make people live a life of complacency versus greatness.

If past disappointments are keeping you from future successes, remember that anyone who has ever accomplished anything has also bombed many times. The sad truth is that you don't hear about it. Take Britney Spears for example: Most people think she just showed up one day, an overnight success. While she was only 16 when she hit it big, no one talked about the ten years of failed auditions, money troubles and stress she underwent as a young artist. I am certain that if we talked to Britney, she would have a treasure trove of stories she could tell about the mishaps that came before her success. The important thing is that she didn't let her failures stop her. She learned from them and kept moving forward. She still stumbles today, yet instead of facing her troubles alone, she has to do it in front of the whole world. Imagine how difficult that must be, yet she keeps moving forward and for that, I applaud her.

You have to decide whether your dreams are more important than your pride. So what if you failed yesterday or might fail tomorrow? Who is going to really know or even care? I have failed many times and not once has anyone ever rubbed it in my face. Most people admire me for trying. My brother Todd used to say to me, "You are so naïve to failure. You just get back up, brush off the dirt and keep moving." It's true. Failure never feels good but that is where life's greatest lessons come from. If you are not failing, you are not trying hard enough. You must step outside your comfort zone from time to time. So Girlfriend, if you have failed at anything in life, realize that you are now more prepared to take the next test. Make it a point to learn the lesson and move on.

> **THINK LIKE THIS GIRL**
>
> *If you don't learn from your mistakes, the tests will only continue to get harder.*

As you pursue the life you want to live, not the one you get, imagine how good it will feel to be free of the past. Now that you've thought about those things that you want to forget, let's take a moment and think about the moments you want to remember. What memories do you have that you can use as rocket fuel, and that will carry you through tough times going forward? If you're like most people it's much easier to remember the bad. It's okay. We are working on changing your thinking. With each day, focus on the good and what you want. These thoughts will outweigh what it is you don't want. Free your mind and give yourself the gift of remembering some of your best memories.

I'll start:

» The evening I received a phone call telling me I had made the cheerleading squad for the first time. I was in the sixth grade, going into seventh, and it completely changed the course of my life. My brother Todd rolled on the floor screaming and crying, he was so happy for me. My mom cried her eyes out because, although she had told me over and over to go for it and that I could do anything I set my mind to, she wasn't quite sure it was true. (She later told me she was shocked I made the squad because usually only the socially prominent girls were chosen in our town.)

» The day I made varsity cheerleading as a sophomore, one of only two in our school history to do so. We were so poor that my mom used nail polish to paint my tennis shoes maroon and white because I couldn't afford the ones I needed for tryouts. That day, I learned I could do anything no matter what the circumstances.

» The day I received a phone call while exiting a rental car bus on a business trip. Someone wanted to publish my first book, *7 Steps to Successful Selling*, and the offer even included a $15,000 advance. I almost fell down the bus's exit stairs!

I have many wonderful memories, many of them personal and close to my heart. These memories, in particular, remind me of my power and prove that I am worthy and do matter.

YOUR TURN

What are some of your best memories?

____

____

____

____

____

____

Who has always believed in you no matter what?

____

____

____

What was the greatest accomplishment of your life so far? What are you most proud of?

What is the kindest thing anyone has ever said to you?

THINK LIKE THIS GIRL

You're going to be here in ten years. You might as well be here doing what you want to do, when you want to do it, on your own terms.

THINK DIFFERENTLY

Each time a bad memory or thought comes to mind, no matter how difficult, I want you to replace it with a good memory or thought. This won't be easy at first but the more often you do it, the easier it will get. It's like starting a new workout routine. In the beginning, lifting just ten pounds is hard. Yet a month into your regime, lifting 20 is easy.

You can train your mind just as you train your muscles. To do this you must be consistent and conscious. Remember, you are fighting for your life.

Here are a few examples:

OLD THOUGHT	NEW THOUGHT
I don't deserve to make a lot of money	If someone's going to make six figures, it might as well be me
My marriage is over	My marriage is improving every day
I don't have time to exercise	I am making exercise a priority
I make just enough to pay the bills	I welcome abundance
I'll always be fat	I am moving toward my ideal health and weight
I have no self-control	I am in control of my life

THINK LIKE THIS GIRL

Change your thoughts and change the course of your life.

A NEW BEGINNING

If you could do anything, what would it be? Stop right now and think about this for a moment. In fact, go ahead and write it down!

____

____

____

If you had a crystal ball and could see ten years into the future, what are the odds you'd be doing that? Tough question, isn't it? As you read this book you will come to know with confidence that you can do anything you set your mind to. You will realize that success is available to everyone, no matter where she comes from. You will know that it's finally your turn to walk through the door of opportunity. In this life, you see the good and pay no mind to the bad. You are in complete control of your thoughts, actions *and results.* You are a positive role model for those around you and give others the confidence to believe that they too can live the life of their dreams. You are confident, balanced, and happy. There is nothing you want for and no life you'd exchange your life for.

PURGE LIKE THIS GIRL:
Chapter Summary

1. No matter what the barrier is, you'll break through and transform your life. No problem is too big, no solution too small. You will do what it takes because the reward is worth it. Your life is on the line.

2. Everyone has a past. Learn from the good, forget the bad and begin to put focus on the future and the life you wish to create.

3. Over time women have become responsible for juggling two full time jobs: Our families and our careers. It's nearly impossible to manage both perfectly, by yourself, and live a life of happiness. You have to make a choice about how you will live and what you can honestly handle. You must commit to doing something about the chaos—or live a life of regrets.

4. You are what you think. Transform your thoughts and transform your life. Pay close attention to your thoughts and revise them if necessary to put the focus on what you want. With each correction, you will gain more control over your mind and will control it versus having it controlling you.

5. If you are not failing, you are not trying hard enough.

chapter three

THINK

BRING ON THAT BRAIN POWER!

I'm fairly certain that the young mother married just eight years, with three children, a German shepherd named Prince and a beautiful home on a quiet street in Springfield, Ohio never dreamed her marriage would end in divorce. As she rocked and sang her babies to sleep, she could not have imagined that one day her family would be torn apart. That instead of dropping her kids at school, preparing delicious meals, running baths and snuggling up for story time, she'd be working three jobs, marrying again in an effort to survive, and moving every six months because she couldn't pay the rent. She couldn't have known that her eldest son, just 11, would move out of state to be with his dad and she would not see him again until he was a young man, serving in the Marines. She had no clue that her second son would leave at 12 to be with his brother and that he too would not come home for close to a decade. Of her three children, she would only get to watch her youngest, her little girl, grow up.

Like many women, this woman's life started off in one direction, then slowly detoured into one she no longer recognized. Bit by bit, each negative experience stole a piece of who she was. Her girl?

Slowly but surely she disappeared. Instead of looking forward and imagining all the possibility, the woman looked ahead and worried about the next possible calamity. Life had failed her and along the way she gave up on any hope of happiness.

The young mother was my mom. The life she set out to live was definitely not the one she got. With each passing year she lost a little bit more of who she was. Bills and letdowns, one after the other, replaced her earlier hopes and dreams. Instead of living her life, she found herself simply trying to survive.

THINK LIKE THIS GIRL

Our dreams are a size too big so we can grow into them.

GIVE IT ANOTHER SHOT

How many women have found themselves in similar situations? Perhaps you are one of them. Although my mom turned her life around and is thriving today, I am certain that those past insecurities creep up every now and then and cause her to second-guess her place in life.

What about you? What has happened in your life to crush your ability to dream big? Maybe you're like my mom, and feel guilty, ashamed and insecure about your broken dreams. I get it. You're only human. But what I want you to know—and what your girl knows—is that no matter how hard you try, you can't change the past. Rather than give yesterday the power over today or your future, use the lessons learned from those challenges and give your dreams another shot. Haven't you sacrificed enough? It's time to get back in the driver's seat!

> THINK LIKE THIS GIRL
>
> *There's enough for everyone, including you! If someone is going to have extreme success, why shouldn't it be you?*

BRAIN GAMES

I am blessed with this incredibly delicious life because I dared to dream big and dream wild. Don't get me wrong, I've had my share of failures. But that doesn't stop me from continuing to think big and go after absolutely everything I want. You know what? The best scenario is that I get what I want. Worst scenario? I don't get what I want. I've never had it anyway, so the reality is that I have everything to gain and nothing to lose simply by trying. You know what else? With the help of my girl, I've learned not to care what other people think. She doesn't. Never did. She reminds me all the time: This is our life and nobody else's!

Here's something else you need to know. The more dreams you have and the more often you take action toward them, the quicker they'll come true. Your successes will build your confidence and courage. From there you'll have bigger visions and be ready to take greater risks—and pretty soon you've got a wonderful snowball effect. (Your girl *loves* snowballs, right?) Over time you begin to understand that the size and scope of the dream is irrelevant. Anything is possible so long as you believe and take action. As you do this you will start to enter an entirely new realm of living. Rather than reacting to circumstances and accepting whatever comes to you, you will live proactively and get exactly what you want out of life.

It can be confusing at first to know what actions to take. This is where the experiments I call "Brain Games" come in. Intrigued by the power of goal setting, I decided to test the limits of my mind. I started with small, insignificant things such as finding my car keys or locating a missing shoe. Rather than run all over looking for them, I would say, "Brain, show me my keys please, I need them now." To make it a real experiment, I decided it was important to let the request go and to trust the mind 100% to do its job. Meaning (in this example) I could not keep looking for them or trying to remember where I put them. Instead, I would go about what I was doing, whether it be putting a bag together, throwing dishes in the dishwasher, or loading up the car. Every time, I found the missing item within minutes. Doing these experiments over and over, I realized that the secret to success is giving control of my life over to the mind and trusting that what I've asked for will be realized. What started out as small things like car keys has transformed into big things like doubling annual sales in my business.

The ultimate proof came when I inserted Brain Games into my business model. At the time my business was generating approximately $50,000 per quarter, or $200,000 in annual revenue. I decided that instead of $50,000 in sales I would sell $100,000 the next quarter. A visual person, I took a bank deposit slip and inscribed on it the date of my goal and the amount of $100,000 in sales for July 1 to October 31, 2007. I didn't know how I was going to do it and I did not care. It was up to my mind to figure out how to make it happen. I gave the goal to my mind and set about doing what I always did in my business. In the picture below you can see what happened. Each time a contract was closed I posted it as a deposit on the slip.

Instead of $100,000, I hit $154,000! All I could think was, "Wow, can it really be this easy?" When I say easy, what I am referring to is the age-old adage, "Ask and ye shall receive." I was using the God-given tool I was born with to direct and design my life according to my deepest desires.

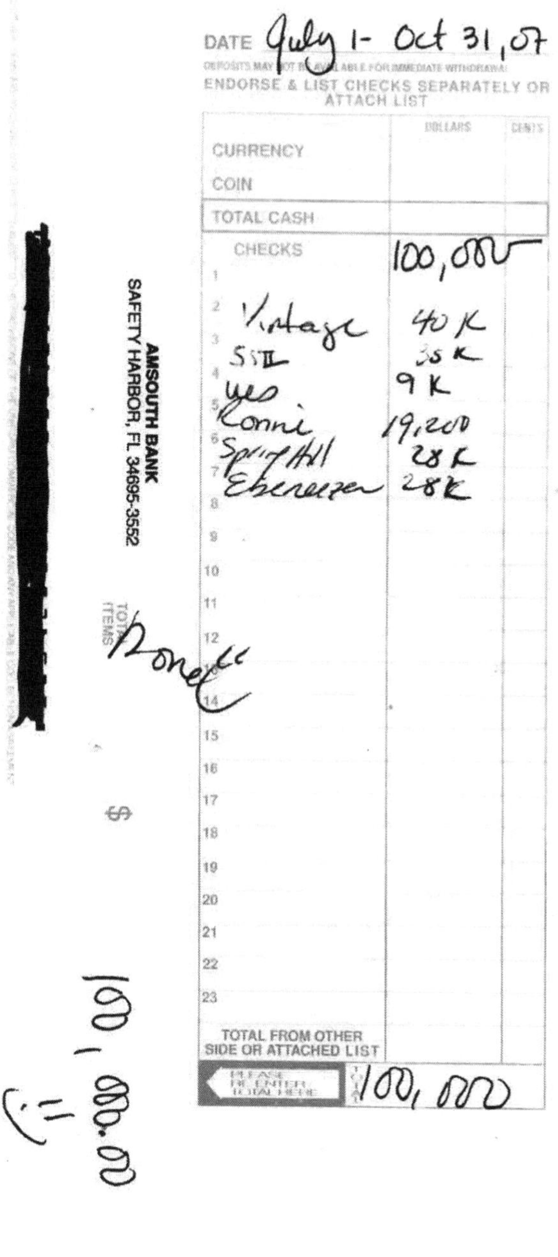

DATE July 1- Oct 31, 07

DEPOSITS MAY NOT BE AVAILABLE FOR IMMEDIATE WITHDRAWAL

ENDORSE & LIST CHECKS SEPARATELY OR ATTACH LIST

	DOLLARS	CENTS
CURRENCY		
COIN		
TOTAL CASH		
CHECKS	100,000	
1		
2 Vintage	40 K	
3 SSII	35 K	
4 Wes	9 K	
5 Ronnie	19,200	
6 Spring Hill	28 K	
7 Ebenezer	28 K	
8		
9		
10		
11		
12		
13		
14		
15		
16		
17		
18		
19		
20		
21		
22		
23		
TOTAL FROM OTHER SIDE OR ATTACHED LIST		
PLEASE RE-ENTER TOTAL HERE — TOTAL	100,000	

AMSOUTH BANK
SAFETY HARBOR, FL 34695-3552

[redacted]

TOTAL ITEMS Ronell

$ 100,000.00 :-)

I did many Brain Games over the next several years. Below is another example of a Brain Game that was impossible in technical terms. My business had never generated this kind of revenue but I decided to run another test. I knew that if I hit $300,000 in a single quarter it was absolutely due to the power of my mind and the absolute control I had over it. Below is the actual deposit slip.

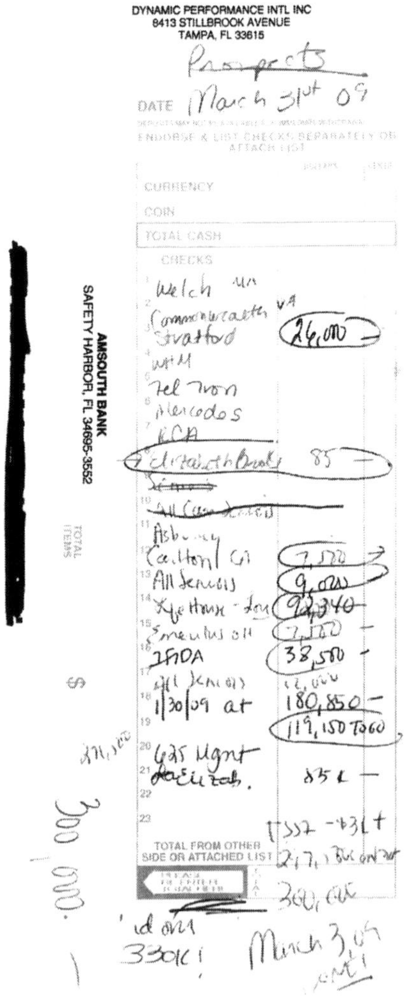
DYNAMIC PERFORMANCE INTL INC
8413 STILLBROOK AVENUE
TAMPA, FL 33615

Prospects

DATE March 31st 09

ENDORSE & LIST CHECKS SEPARATELY OR ATTACH LIST

CURRENCY

COIN

TOTAL CASH

CHECKS

26,000

85

7,500

9,000

92,340

7,500

38,500

180,850

119,150 To go

TOTAL FROM OTHER SIDE OR ATTACHED LIST

300,000

March 3, 09

AMSOUTH BANK
SAFETY HARBOR, FL 34695-3552

TOTAL ITEMS

$

[redacted]

300,000.

As you can see, my mind over-delivered again by exceeding $330,000 in sales in one quarter. At the conclusion of these experiments I decided never to question the power of my mind again. Oddly enough, the difficultly in this type of goal setting is not the physical task of accomplishing the goal but instead trusting yourself enough to believe you can do it and that your mind will attract the tools, resources and people needed to make the goals a reality.

As you work to get your girl back, I want to impart how important it is to start using the full capacity of your mind. There may be a situation that seems impossible or a problem that is so big you are certain there is no rational solution. Yet if you give it over to the mind and request a resolution or a solution, trusting that it will come, it will. I have learned that the greatest asset I have is my mind. It was God who said, "You can move a mountain." (Matthew 17:20, author's paraphrase) It was man who said, "How?" Stop asking how and give up trying to understand how it works. You cannot see air, but you breathe it every moment. Electricity is not visible to the naked eye, but it powers lights that allow you to read at night. Just know this and be thankful.

This is a lot to take in, especially if you have never tapped into this inner power. I challenge you to start small like I did. Build your faith with small Brain Games until you are ready to move into the bigger life-changing ones. The next time you are panicked and running around looking for something or attempting to hit a month-end goal at work, stop and play a Brain Game. Ask your mind to show you where the item you are looking for is: "Brain, show me my shoes, I need them now." If it's the end of the month and you are far from hitting your goal, stop and say, "Brain, I need to hit this month-end goal. Bring me the tools and resources needed to make this goal a reality." Go about your day and every so often restate what you need your mind to do for you. Trust that you will get what you want and remember that the mind is smart and knows if you are second-guessing it. So don't!

I have tried to teach this to my nine-year-old daughter, Paris. It's not an easy concept to grasp, as society has taught us to expect instant results. You have to practice. Imagine learning something new such as rollerblading. Odds are it will take a little trial and error and a lot of effort before you trust your ability to head out for a two-mile ride. The same holds true with Brain Games. Experiment and test the limits of your mind. Let your confidence grow by achieving success with small things and gradually begin to build into bigger ones.

If it were not for the power of my mind I would not be where I am today. While some would say I got lucky in life, I know that my life was purposely directed and I instead simply got what I asked for. The more Brain Games you play, the more in tune you become to the power your mind holds over reality.

THINK LIKE THIS GIRL

You can think your dreams into reality.

As you begin to reflect on the power of Brain Games, consider the impact they'll have on your life to "order up" anything your heart desires: Private schools or college for your children, travel, a new home, funds for your favorite charity, a funded retirement, and more.

Take a moment and jot down dreams that lurk in your mind. Don't think about whether you can accomplish them or how. Just put pen to paper and have fun:

____

____

____

THINK LIKE THIS GIRL

Trust your mind. It knows how to take you where you want to go and can take you there, if you'll let it.

MENTAL PROGRAMMING

It's not easy to believe in yourself, and it may be even harder to imagine that you were born for something great. Each of you was programmed differently by your past. Because my life was difficult growing up, my mom went out of her way to encourage me and remind me that my life could be different from hers. As a result, I became programmed to believe that nothing was impossible. I never doubted my ability for a moment and am living proof that we are what we think we are. Sadly, many parents fail to do for their children what my mother did for me. Instead of praise, positive reinforcement and encouragement, many children receive words of negativity and even abuse. Perhaps this happened to you.

The mental programming you received as a child is more than likely evident in your life as an adult today. If you don't like the current state of your life or how you feel, begin the transformation by changing your thought process. While not easy to do, reprogramming your mind will allow you to override negative thoughts with positive ones and put focus on what you want versus what you don't want.

THINK LIKE THIS GIRL

You are going to be here in one, five, or ten years. You might as well be here doing what you want to do.

GIVE THE BRAIN A JOB

To achieve what you want in life you must gain mental focus. This means gaining control of your thoughts. The human brain produces approximately 70,000 thoughts a day and those tend to gravitate toward the negative. You must retrain your mind with positive thoughts, repeating them over and over, one at a time. Like I said earlier, it's just like training your muscles. Lots of reps required!

Reflect on a time in your life when you felt the most confident, vibrant and certain. This is the mental state you seek. Getting your girl back, more than anything, is a state of mind. It is operating from a place of mental power and control.

What was your girl like, how did people respond to her, and how did she feel? The more you think about her, the sooner she will begin to reappear. Remember that your brain wants a job. It will literally do whatever you tell it to do. How many times have you said to yourself, "Don't eat that cookie!" Yet within five minutes you are eating the cookie. All the brain hears is, "Eat cookie." Researchers have found that that's the way the brain works. It doesn't hear the "don't!"

How *This* Girl Does It: *Michele Hockwalt*

My mother was amazing. She instilled in me a real passion for reading and learning. I was very shy in school, but my teachers saw something in me, and always identified me as a "smart girl." In college, I started taking classes to become an attorney when I realized, *This is the worst career ever for me. I'll be surrounded by negativity all the time.* I ended up with a history and political science degree and thought, *now what?* I had a great group of strong, smart girlfriends who knew what they wanted. They taught me, "It's okay to take risk. It's okay to be in touch with who you are."

For awhile, I managed and developed teams, running meetings and lecturing. I was successful, but I felt there was no room to grow, and left to pursue an MBA. I knew I needed to follow my passion for educating people. In my position now, I make a difference in people's lives, harness my creativity, travel, speak and educate. I have a sense of real accomplishment.

My girl was always eager to find her happiness, but didn't know what it was. She was eager to be successful, and be respected, but she didn't know what that looked like. She was eager to be perceived as intelligent and generous to those around her in the community, but didn't know what direction to take. My girl had dreams, but they were never defined. I found her at 38, and now that I know what I want, I go after it and give it everything I've got.

Have you ever wondered why you gain weight when dieting, break out before an important event, or arrive late to catch an important flight? Subconsciously, your mind will focus on the words you say, and because it wants a job, like most organs in your body, it will do what you tell it to do. For example, when dieting, people are consumed with thoughts of losing and not gaining weight. All day long thoughts of weight occupy their minds: Don't eat that chocolate, don't drink that soda, don't eat that bag of chips, and so on. But all the mind hears is, eat chocolate, drink soda, and eat chips. Because there is so much emphasis on weight, the mind thinks, "Weight, weight, weight." The result is, you gain weight rather than lose it.

In contrast, using the same example, it would be more effective to focus on ideal health. Fuel your mind with those things that result in great health and let these thoughts consume your mind instead: Eat fruits and vegetables, exercise and drink lots of water. What the mind hears is eat fruits and vegetables, drink water and exercise. Because there is so much emphasis on health, it thinks, "Health, health, health." The result is, you get healthy. Pay close attention to your word choices. Give your brain very clear and concise directions by focusing on the outcome you want.

When negative thoughts pop up—and they will—restate them in a way that focuses on what you want instead. Here are a few examples to get you started:

WHAT YOU DON'T WANT	WHAT YOU WANT
I am 30 pounds overweight. I'll never be that girl again.	I am fit and healthy.
How am I supposed to have time to dance when all I do is work?	I want to dance again and feel the music.
I've been married 16 years. I don't even know my husband anymore.	I am crazy in love with my husband.
I'm just a taxi cab driver with three kids who don't appreciate me.	I love being a mom and choose to be their driver.
I hate all these wrinkles. Who am I?	I'm blessed that I am here to see these lines appear.

THINK LIKE THIS GIRL

We are what we think we are, so be careful what you think.

Your mind is like a computer and it's your job to give it new programming. Rephrase your word choices when necessary. The more you do this, the faster your mind will work as you want it to. Be patient and realize that you have decades of programming to change. Know that with each statement of what you want rather than what you don't, you'll feel more empowered and in control of your life.

DIRECT YOUR THOUGHTS

Make up your mind to consciously direct your thoughts. When they stray, force them back where you want them. Remember, just as you are what you eat, you are what you think. As you look in the mirror, find something you like instead of something you hate. When you go to the closet to pick out an outfit, focus on finding something you love instead of complaining that you don't have anything to wear. Instead of yelling at your kids that they are going to be late, try saying, "Hurry up kids, we want to be on time today." These are very subtle changes, but they will have incredible impact

HOW *THIS* GIRL DOES IT: KATHY BRENTLINGER

I have always been intentional about being a positive thinker. I am on guard against negativity. I am very diligent about keeping a good attitude. I read books and listen to DVDs that I know will impact me in a positive way. To this day, I am a note taker. I love to learn. My morning routine is tuning into Joyce Meyer daily and taking notes. Then I review the notes on the weekend and reflect on what I have learned.

on your life. Control of your thoughts is essential to getting your girl back. It takes confidence and courage to create a life that is extraordinary. There will be many obstacles, distractions and fearful moments. Control of your thoughts will allow you to navigate these challenges and stay on course.

My life has been filled with evidence of the power of the mind. At an early age I made a point of figuring out what I wanted in life: To be a motivational speaker, to have a beautiful home on the water, to drive a nice car, to travel the world and to have a refrigerator full of food. On the next page is a picture of a boat I put in my dream journal 15 years before it actually came into my life. I vividly remember cutting this picture out and placing it into the second page of my journal. It was such a farfetched idea that I would have a boat like this, but putting it in my book made it feel like a real possibility. My mind took note and held onto this dream because my first boat was the exact same color, size and type. The only difference was the year of the model. Doesn't this look like further proof that the mind is in the driver's seat and will help you get exactly what you want?

Dream Boat

Actual Boat

THINK LIKE THIS GIRL

Bottle the passion of your girl and take a drink from it every morning.

TRACI WHO?

The earliest love letter I found that fateful day in 2011 was dated December, 1992. My name was not Traci Bild then. It was Traci Shafer. Traci Shafer. Wow, I haven't said that name in a long time. Today I am Traci Bild, wife of David Bild. I have two amazing children, Paris and Noah, and a wildly successful business as a motivational speaker. I live on the water in Clearwater, Florida, have a Mercedes and a Porsche, and I've traveled all over the world: Italy, France, Great Britain, Germany, Switzerland, and more. I have a refrigerator full of food and I have a business I love.

I guess you could say I got what I asked for. My mother always told me, "Be careful what you ask for, you just might get it." Today, as Traci Bild, I know this is true. Perhaps that is why at 42, I am much more discerning about the goals I set and the things I ask for. I know that, with each request, there is a price. As you begin to grasp the power you have to attract what you want, be cognizant of the speed in which you want it to come. The mind is powerful and responds quickly to specific commands. Think big thoughts but first think through what you want and why you want it. Each year I take the time to ponder what I want and why I want it. I can attest that this is time well spent.

THINK LIKE THIS GIRL

No person and no material item can bring you happiness. True happiness comes from the inside and that can only be achieved by maintaining balance in your life.

PURGING GUILT

Over the past 20 years I've talked with thousands of women from all walks of life. And what I've found is that the number one barrier to getting your girl back is unnecessary guilt. I'm not talking about the kind where you really did something mean or criminal. I'm talking about that pervasive sense that you've done something wrong, a sense that is not grounded in anything specific or real. Guilt is a powerful emotion and can color every decision in your life if you let it. Women in particular wrestle with it daily. Employed moms often feel guilty for getting work tasks done when they're with the kids, and then feel guilty at work for not being with the kids! And how about this one: Have you ever bought something for yourself and felt like you had just committed a cardinal sin? Have you ever *not* felt guilty about treating yourself? Guilt—it's always there, poking you in the chest, reminding you that you are a horrible person.

For many, guilt can be all-consuming. And we don't just do it to ourselves. Sometimes it is inflicted on us by a parent, child, partner, boss or friend. Whatever the source, your girl doesn't need to be beaten down like that. Nobody does! Moving forward, when guilt shows up, change your focus to what you want and the outcome you seek. It takes incredible mental strength and focus to overcome this powerful emotion. But it can be done! I know that, because I've done it.

OH, LORD, WON'T YOU BUY ME A MERCEDES BENZ?

I wasn't always so gracious about having dreams come true. Not long ago Dave and I went to pick up a new Mercedes that we purchased for the family. I struggled with this purchase. I knew we could afford it. That wasn't the problem. No, I felt overwhelmed by what people might think and wondered whether it looked like too much when we already had a Porsche sitting in the garage. I could afford to pay cash for the car and had taken risks others would not have even considered to earn that money. Still, when the reward stood right in front of me, I could barely fake a smile.

As we pulled into the dealership, I felt tears welling up. I tried to hide them from Dave because this was supposed to be a big moment and I didn't want to ruin it. I put a smile on my face and ran through the new car drill. I looked inside, outside, and pretended interest by asking questions. As I climbed into the driver's seat and grabbed hold of the wheel, I looked over at Dave and realized that no matter how hard I tried to cover my dismay, he clearly sensed it. As we drove off, he called me out. "What's wrong?" he asked. I told him I was consumed by guilt. We talked it through. And with Dave's loving encouragement, that day I decided I'd never again feel guilty for my success. My decision has been incredibly freeing and has given me an entirely new perspective on life. With time and practice, it can be the same for you.

Consider the role guilt plays in your own life. List some things you feel guilty about, either from your past or your present.

____

____

____

____

Now make a list of things you've avoided because doing or having them would make you feel guilty.

How do you feel as you write these things down? Do you see how guilt has held you back?

Now write a little bit about what your life would be like if you didn't feel guilty about things that weren't mean or criminal—things where you really didn't do anything wrong.

Letting go of guilt will not happen overnight. It is going to take a concentrated effort to keep your mind positive and away from thoughts that you don't deserve the best, but the freedom it brings will be well worth the effort. With a newfound awareness of your thought process and the power of your mind, you will get your girl back and keep her for the long haul. You are slowly introducing the girl of yesterday to the woman of today to create a sense of unity and power unlike anything you have ever experienced.

THINK LIKE THIS GIRL:
Chapter Summary

1. You're not only allowed to start dreaming again, you're required! Before you got married, had children, started a career and became all things to all people, there was plenty of time to dream, set goals and take action on them. Yet as time passed and responsibility set in, those dreams and goals gave way to the needs of your children, partner, job, PTA, and more. Not knowing better, you put your dreams on hold and forgot to hit play. Now, a few years or even decades later, you feel the loss of your girl and the dreams she had. You are going to dare to dream again. Do not worry about how or whether you will accomplish your dreams, just take the first step of being willing.

2. People naturally think of the things they don't want, can't have or can't do. This is how we are all programmed by our parents and other influential people. It's common to use negative language as we try to move through our days. Program your mind: You can't do anything about the past, but you can reshape the future by reprogramming your mind and putting focus on the positive—on things you want, can do and will have.

3. Your life is the result of your thoughts. To bring change to any area of your life, change your thoughts. Direct them. Focus on your thoughts and watch for patterns that drag you down. When you hear yourself think about something you don't want, restate it to something you do want. Each time you do this you will grow in power and move closer to finding your girl.

THINK LIKE THIS GIRL:

Chapter Summary

(Continued)

4. As a young woman, it was probably much easier to set goals and dreams. As you age, responsibilities increase and you sacrifice so many of your own wants and needs that before you know it you are in survival mode. That is no way to live. You deserve to thrive.

5. The brain wants work to do. Give it the task of getting you what you want and simply ignore what you don't want. Train your brain like you train your body. Lots of repetitions!

chapter four

FOCUS

GO AHEAD, MAKE IT ALL ABOUT YOU!

While on vacation with my family, I found myself wandering through the most enchanting gardens. With each turn I encountered a new surprise: A large purple hydrangea, a bluebell flower the most exquisite blue you can imagine, orange lilies the size of my hand, and scents that just filled me up. Bumblebees and butterflies hovered and swirled around the blossoms as if they were dancing to music that only they could hear. With each new discovery, my heart leapt with joy.

Where did I find this Eden? I was in Claude Monet's garden in Giverny, France. This was the same garden the artist strolled through three times a day to find inspiration for his work, including his famous Water Lily series. As I approached the legendary lily ponds he designed, then painted so brilliantly, I felt the sting of tears. I was walking in Claude Monet's footsteps. These were the flowers he planted, the benches he sat on, the clouds he pondered under, the light he interpreted with such beauty and permanently captured at all different stages of the day.

Although Monet was long gone, I felt his presence. I felt drunk on his genius and could only hope that, in some way, his spirit would guide me closer to my own personal mastery. My Monet experience was life-changing. The mere size of Monet's Water Lily series was an incredible feat and unheard of in his day. His canvas consisted of three panels, each 6′ 6-3/4″ x 13′ 11-1/4″ (200 x 424.8 cm), overall 6′ 6-3/4″ x 41′ 10-3/8″ (200 x 1276 cm). Rather than contemplate the opinions of others, he followed his own instinct and passion and made the decision to do what he felt must be done to manifest his vision. He was not concerned with what his contemporaries were doing, or what they might say about his work; he simply thought of what he wanted to do and did it. The result is history. His paintings have moved millions of people and will continue to do so long after all of us are gone.

This experience also moved me because at one time I believed I'd never get to visit a place so sacred and profound. What were the odds that I, Traci Shafer, from Urbana, Ohio would meander through Monet's gardens in Giverny, France? As much as I believe in, and live by, the power of goals, I am still amazed when they are realized. In truth, I will never get used to it. It was the combination of Monet's dreams as well as my own that rocked my soul. To think that we actually had something in common was intoxicating. We were both dreamers. And you? Are you also a dreamer?

WHAT'S YOUR DREAM?

What do you dream about? At one time or other, most of us have visions of things we secretly desire. Often these dreams come to us when doing things we despise such as housework, going to a dead end job or being stuck in traffic. Mine often appear when I am alone and in some sort of solitude when my mind is free to wonder and think, "What if?"

What do you fantasize about? Take a moment now and just sit. Close your eyes, or stare out the window or at the wall. Let your mind drift for five minutes. Ask yourself, "What do I really want?"

Remember, these are fantasies so you don't have to think about whether you will ever do these things. Don't edit your thoughts based on your past or on your current situation. Do not second-guess yourself. Just dream about what you want, not what you think you can get or would settle for. Let yourself go!

Okay. Now take another five minutes and write everything down. Remember, no editing! No criticism! No judgments! Just write.

Having trouble? To help you get your thoughts flowing, I'll start. Here is what I dream about:

» Sitting in a café in Rome, sipping a cappuccino

» Indulging in a massage while surrounded by candles, enchanting music and the smell of rosemary

» Spending a few hours in a bookstore/coffee shop, browsing while the combined smells of coffee and paper fill me with the desire to learn and grow as a person

You will notice none of my fantasies include my children or husband. Does that make me a bad person? Maybe to some people. The point is that I am being honest with you. I am not trying to be someone I am not nor do I desire to impress you. To get your girl back you have to let go of others' expectations for your life. This has to be about you.

Paradoxically, making yourself the center of your own life actually makes relationships work better. I spend time every day with my family. They understand how much I love and adore them because my actions to help and support them and fill their needs prove it. They are the only people who matter. Yet I refuse to be some sort of self-sacrificing supermom. I won't be a martyr who does nothing for herself. So when I escape, trust me, it's by myself. And when I come back to them, I am refreshed and renewed, and we are all the better for it.

Who were you before you had the weight of the world on your shoulders? You must learn to separate who you were, who you are, and who you want to become. That amazing human being is the girl you were born to be. Whether you are 20, 40, 60 or 80, you have a young, hungry girl inside who wants a life of passion, fun and complete joy. You are on the way to setting her free!

> THINK LIKE THIS GIRL
>
> *Give up worrying about what others think of you. The only people who matter are those who love and understand you and will never judge you. Those individuals know you are doing your best and that is all that matters. You don't have to prove yourself. You're already wonderful!*

FOCUS

Imagine what would happen if you stopped thinking about what you should do and just did what you wanted? I know you need to fulfill certain responsibilities. We all do. But what about that long-deferred class, degree, new business or trip? If responsibilities could be set aside, where would you go, what would you do?

Twelve years ago I told my personal coach, Sue Youngs, that I wanted to live in Europe for a month, sit in cafes and write a new book. I was 30. Two years ago, at 40, I went to my husband and told him I wanted to spend the following summer in Paris. We had taken several short trips, but never for this length of time. Dave's immediate response was "Okay, crazy lady!" I was grateful he didn't stand in the way, but I'll tell you something, Girlfriends! I was going, one way or the other!

I began making plans. Not surprisingly, people started telling me all the ways this trip wouldn't work: My kids were too young. The trip was too long. I couldn't run my business from Paris. Yet I knew what I wanted. For ten years I craved living like a Parisian for a month. So I did it! I ignored the naysayers, cashed in my American Express points for four flights and booked an apartment. I knew that I had to make this decision and that no one else could make it for me. How could I expect others to understand what I wanted and why I wanted it? They're not me! I focused on my dream and blocked all those other voices out. It is critical that you do the same.

Standing your ground is not easy. This is why it's so important to get your girl back. She has the grit to make decisions and stand by them. She's bold! As a woman, you know what's best for you and your family. Yet it's very easy to be influenced by others and riddled

How *This* Girl Does It: *Angela Jia Kim*

I don't think I ever experienced my girl to the fullest because of my family's work ethic. I was trained as a classical pianist. I remember at the age of eight or nine preparing for a piano competition. I had a memory slip on stage and forgot some notes. I asked my mother, "It's okay, right? I might get second or third." And she answered, "That's not good enough. You must always be first prize. You can't make mistakes on stage." From then on, I developed a phobia about not being perfect. This completely choked any fun out of what I was doing.

In my early 30s, I made a small mistake during a concert for one of my idols. I remember thinking I was such a failure. When I got on the plane later, my heart was screaming, "Something has got to change. You are not a surgeon, where your patient could die in your hands. You have got to stop taking yourself this seriously." This was my "missed note, missed life" moment. I realized I wasn't living my life in the way that life was meant to be lived. The only way I knew to tell my mom that I was quitting for good was to tell her, "Mom. I know you want a granddaughter. If I'm on the road all of the time, Marc and I won't be able to have a baby." On June 15, 2009, my piano days ended, and four months later, I became a proud mama.

My girl now is an ever-evolving journey. For me, putting energy out and getting that energy back feels like I have my girl everyday. My store, Om Aroma, launched in 2007 in New York City, followed shortly by a boutique spa, Savor Spa. We just opened up our own manufacturing facility, and are also starting our "Dollars & Scents" program for women transitioning in the work force. Savor the Success, a networking group for women entrepreneurs, launched in 2009. I'm also launching the Manifest Method School to really teach women how to have a successful business and life to savor. I have the power back now in my girl!

with guilt over decisions that might seem extravagant or unnecessary. You need your girl because more than likely, the woman you are today is defined by a partner, children, a job, bills, and an endless list of responsibilities. It's not so easy to just do what you want when so many others are involved.

When others stand against you, focus your thoughts on the end goal. Think, "What do I want to achieve?" The more focus you put on your dreams versus what others are saying, the closer you will move toward accomplishing what you set out to do. Life is short. You get one shot. If you are not going to stand up for what you want now, when will you?

A month in Paris was much more to me than a glamorous vacation. It meant learning to speak French, making friends, experiencing the culture, re-living history, indulging in food and in the art of doing nothing. The month in Paris was the trip of a lifetime and I wanted to experience it while I was young and healthy—and most importantly before my kids became so involved in sports and other activities that a month away would become impossible!

So I went to Paris for a month with my family. I walked in the footsteps of Claude Monet, traced my fingers along Rodin's signature on his famous sculpture The Thinker, drank in real Picasso paintings, followed in Hemingway's footsteps, dined in a chateau and sipped cappuccinos in sidewalk cafés.

THINK LIKE THIS GIRL

If you don't pursue your dreams right now, you may not get another chance. What are you waiting for?

I want you to know that pursuing this dream took effort. But every failure, defeat and ounce of sweat was more than worth it. I have taken lots of risks in my life and stepped off many a cliff, yet the rewards have been tenfold. While others tell you to be cautious, not to set your sights too high for fear of being let down, or that you already have more than you need, I am going to tell you the opposite. Throw caution to the wind, go for your dreams and make them big. Who cares if you fail? You can get back up and try again. Yes, you may have what you need. But do you have what you want?

What's one thing you'd like to do but have put off because it seemed too selfish?

____

____

____

____

____

THINK LIKE THIS GIRL

You have everything to gain and nothing to lose by going after your dreams. Whatever you desire, you don't have it now, so if you fail, who cares? You've lost nothing! If you succeed? Imagine what you will gain! There is nothing more intoxicating than living a dream that you manifest with your own sheer will and determination.

DEFINE

Each experience I share with you is a result of an earlier dream I created in my thoughts. Very little has happened by chance. It took me ten years to get to Paris for a month. Each time you accomplish something that once seemed impossible, it becomes easier and easier to accomplish something else. You may be afraid to state your dreams out loud for fear they may not become reality. You may feel ashamed for even having the dreams that are in your heart. Perhaps your parents raised you to believe that thinking big was selfish or greedy and that you needed to live your life for others. As women, we have been brainwashed to believe that our sole purpose is to serve others. Don't get me wrong, I do a lot for others! As a wife, mother, daughter, friend, business owner and more, I do a lot of giving and I love every minute of it. What I have learned, though, is that I must also give to myself.

Let's focus on your thought patterns:

- You are allowed to think of yourself and even put yourself first at times.
- It is okay to dream big.
- It is not wrong to want nice things such as a beautiful home, a pool, a luxurious car, nice perfume or a beautiful silk dress.
- It is not true that if you obtain the material items you want you'll lose the things you hold most dear.

> THINK LIKE THIS GIRL
>
> *Fear is nothing more than an illusion. Don't let it steal your dreams.*

PLAN

To move forward, get your girl back and experience a life that is beyond your greatest expectations and far beyond the life you are living today, you must take the time to develop your plan. What is it you want for yourself that is indulgent and self-serving? I know I asked you this already. This time around, I want you to think bigger and dig deeper. I want you to ponder a life of abundance.

Perhaps you have been living paycheck to paycheck and are tired of robbing Peter to pay Paul. Do you dream of a day when money no longer controls your every thought? What impact would it have on your life if you made double or even triple what you make now? How would it feel to go to the grocery and be able to purchase what you want versus what you can afford? What impact would it make on your state of mind to have a housekeeper clean your home every week? How much better would you sleep if you had six months of expenses tucked away in a savings account? Allow yourself to consider these thoughts for just a moment.

Maybe finances aren't the problem. Maybe you're dealing with poor health. What impact would it have on your life if one year from today you were at your ideal body weight, exercised daily, ate healthy, slept through the night, had high energy levels and could put on a bathing suit without being filled with dread?

You know what you want. Your girl is nudging you right now. She wants you to speak your truth and claim what is rightfully yours. No one is here but you. In a minute, I'm going to ask you to write down your vision. To help you get started, I'll go first. Please take note that I am not afraid to think big. This takes courage and time so don't beat yourself up if you struggle a bit with the guilt. I did for years.

I want a pool installed behind my home, a new boat with an extra cabin for the kids, a golf cart so I can take the children out at night to get ice cream and cruise the streets looking for fun while

Christmas lights dangle off the cart and illuminate the streets. I want to write books from exotic places all over the world while my children study cultures they've only read about in books. I want to have my nine-year-old daughter, Paris, take $500 and sponsor ten women in a microloan program in a developing country so she can see the impact a small difference can make. My selfish end goal? To teach her the art and power in giving and effecting change. There is much more I want to do, this is just what comes to mind right now.

Your turn. What are your wants, dreams, wishes, and goals?

Now, rather than just thinking of what you want in general, let's break things down a bit more. Let's consider the compartments of your life.

LET'S TALK CAREER

What would you do, if you could have any career at all? What's your gift—the very thing that people always say you are so incredible at doing? What gives you sheer joy when you do it and is something you love so much that you would do it for free? When I first started speaking in public, I loved it so much I did it for free. I didn't have an end objective in mind, I just knew more than anything else in the world that I wanted to be a professional speaker like my mentors before me.

Trust me when I say I had no idea how I was going to do it. My first couple of speaking opportunities went so well that when I asked for referrals I got them. Initially, as I spoke more and more, I never received a dime. My payment was the smiling faces in the audience, the joy I felt at getting my message out, and the sense of accomplishment I garnered at actually having something to say.

One day a woman who wanted me to speak to her organization asked what my fee was. "$500," I said. To my amazement, she said, "Well, that's a deal, we'll book you." I couldn't believe that someone would pay me that much for talking! Not long after, I was charging $25 per person and presenting public seminars where I sold my business book in the back of the room. Things evolved. Then there was the time I was presenting in front of a very large audience in Las Vegas and I heard a man ask my husband what my fee was. Dave responded, "$5,000." The gentleman said, "Great, I'd like to book her." I almost passed out. Now some of my seminars bring in $10,000. All for doing what I love.

What I learned is, when you do what you love, success comes much easier than when you do something you have to do just to get by. By following my passion, I have earned more money than I ever dreamed possible. The craziest thing is that I still would do it for free. And I do sometimes speak for free. So what would you do for free, if given the opportunity to do it as a career? Use my story to stimulate your own thoughts. Think without limits and don't think about the "how to" part, we'll get to that. Do not worry about what your parents, spouse, friends, current business associates or anyone else will think or say, this is your time to extract your dream and yours alone.

What would you do in your career if you could do anything at all? What gift do you have that you can utilize? What brings you sheer joy?

LET'S TALK RELATIONSHIPS

We're going to get more personal now. Are you single, married or widowed? Are you where you want to be? If you have a significant other, is it the relationship you always dreamed about? This is a time to be honest with yourself—no shame allowed! You need to be real with your emotions.

The number one goal in my life is to stay married to Dave. While others may not understand this, to me it solves a world of problems. If Dave and I stay married, our children will have the consistent, solid family foundation I never had. I made a vow to love Dave until death do us part, for better or worse, in sickness and in health. Dave has been an incredibly good husband and has never given me cause to consider leaving him. My opinion has always been that marriage is not easy but that it's easier with Dave than it would be with anyone else because of our history and our children. No matter how hard it gets, I might as well work it out with him. Seriously, if it's hard with the spouse you have, who is vested in your life, imagine how hard marriage is to someone new who is not? I applaud people who can make marriage work because statistics show the odds are against them.

Perhaps you have been divorced or remarried. Trust me, I do not judge. Some marriages simply do not work and some people marry for the wrong reasons and, in some situations, it is downright unhealthy to stay. Personally, I am in a good marriage. The fact is I've invested a lot of time and energy into making my marriage great. I have many friends who are in loveless marriages, friends who are no longer intimate with their partners, or who have completely different interests. These are big red flags to me. I've made it my business to pay very close attention to my marriage and to give it the time, energy and effort needed for it to succeed. This doesn't mean we don't have bumps in the road, because we do. Yet I have systems that ensure when those bumps arise, I can maneuver over them. I'll address these important systems later in the book. Right now, take some time to think about the relationship you would have if anything were possible. I know you can't change your partner, but you can change yourself and that is always the best start. If you are single, you have a fresh clean slate!

If you could wake up tomorrow and have the relationship you wanted, what would it be like, how would it feel, and what would it do for you? If you are not in a relationship at all, but desire one, what would it look and feel like?

____

____

____

____

LET'S TALK HEALTH

Health! Oh, this is such a touchy subject! I'm 42 and I want to stay healthy, using ideas, values and strategies that make me feel good about myself. My metabolism has clearly slowed down and it seems that anything I eat goes directly to my muffin top. That said, I've allowed myself to create the health and physique that is acceptable to me. The media may tell me I should be a size 0, but I realize that at 42, with two kids and a career, I will never be teeny-tiny slender. (And, actually, now that I think of it, I've never been a size 0!) My personal goal is to fit into my size 6 jeans and if I can do that, I feel good. There are days when I literally have to jump and squeeze myself into them but so long as they fit, I'm happy. When I do go up to an eight, which I have in my closet, I know it's time to pay attention to my eating and exercise habits. As I kick my exercise up and monitor what I eat, those size 6 jeans begin to slip on again.

I also work hard to eat healthy. My goal is to eat meat no more than once a week and to include more fish and vegetables in the family diet. The better I eat and the more fit I stay, the more energy I have and the better my state of mind. It's a direct correlation. When I focus on health, I get health. Although it's not always easy to focus, you get what you concentrate on. The more you give your energy to what you want, the easier it is to do what's right for yourself.

Now, what about you? What are your health goals? What do you want to feel and look like?

Is that space still blank? Do not skip this step. I don't care if you are 150 pounds overweight. To get where you want to go, you must decide exactly you want. Our culture has made it almost impossible to be healthy. Food is loaded with preservatives, dinner plate sizes are double what they should be and fast food restaurants are placed

How *This* Girl Does It: Vicki Mertin

I didn't realize my girl was lost until I faced a life-changing medical diagnosis. Until that point, I'd been busy with life and hadn't given much thought to health. I was married to my best friend and soul mate. We had five amazing children. I was a stay-at-home mom and was also trying to build an online business. My life consisted of carpooling, helping with homework, volunteering, cooking, cleaning and other household duties. I went to the gym sporadically and worked on my business when I could, but fitness and my personal interests were definitely not priorities. I was too busy taking care of everyone else.

The year I turned 40, I was diagnosed with breast cancer. My only treatment option was a mastectomy. I opted for a double mastectomy with immediate reconstruction. During the year it on every corner of America. I know how difficult it is. That's why I want you to understand that you need more than willpower. You need a very focused plan of what you want. In the second half of this book, I am going to give you systems to help you to get there.

LET'S TALK FINANCES

It's time to move on to your finances. Another difficult subject, but money is part of life and something you must address, particularly as a woman. This subject has to do more with psychology than ability, in my opinion. We have been so brainwashed to believe that it's easier for a rich man to fit through the eye of a needle than to get into heaven that we would rather stay poor, stressed and downright broke. I have met so many women who live with shame and guilt over their desire to be financially successful. They just can't get their brain around having what they need and want. I used to be one of these women—but not anymore.

took me to recover, I had a lot of time to read and reflect. I leaned into God and pursued my relationship with Him. I gained a fresh perspective and started investing in me. I've always had a passion for food and cooking so I learned everything I could about diet and nutrition and how they affect health. I began to incorporate my new knowledge into what I prepared for my family. I started going to the gym regularly and recommitted to building my business. I started investing in me and it felt great!

I am getting my girl back! I prioritize my time, create goals and have started a dream notebook. My husband and I are passionate about investing in our relationship and our children. We volunteer at church, lead a group and invest in building relationships. I begin each day by spending time with God and journaling. I am passionate about growing my business, its mission and how I can impact and influence others. I am investing in myself and the things that matter to me—every day!

> THINK LIKE THIS GIRL
>
> *Jesus was an incredibly wealthy man and from what I understand, he is sitting at the right hand of God. Don't let fear of abundance steal your prosperity.*

Isn't it a bit odd that when a man is financially successful society applauds and admires him? Why is it so different with a woman? Once upon a time, men and women got married and the men worked while the women stayed home and took care of the family. As time passed, divorce rates started to soar, men left, and many failed to provide child support. Women began to enter the work force in massive numbers and take on the role of parent and financial provider. Even so, women have been expected to earn just enough to make ends meet and survive, no more. If that were not the case we would have equality in pay.

This is how I was raised. My mom worked three jobs to provide for my brothers and me. She worked in factories, as a bartender, a waitress, a nurse's aide. I am certain in each job, she made less than her male counterparts. The same thing still goes on today. Well, I can't change pay in America, but I can help you change the way you think and help you get what you want financially. It's time that you were paid what you're worth and that you create a plan to ensure you pay yourself first, before everyone else. To achieve your financial goals, you need money and a plan. I don't know how to say it any other way.

GOAL #1: $600 A MONTH

When Dave and I got married, I was 28 years old. I was in business with my brother Todd, and my financial goal was to make $600 a month—enough to pay the bills. What's crazy is that each month that is exactly what I made: $600. It's amazing how one always gets exactly what she asks for and expects. As you can imagine I continued to raise that goal year after year. Oddly enough, each year I hit the goal or came incredibly close. Even if I didn't hit the goal exactly, I felt that getting close was pretty good, because without that goal I wouldn't have gotten close at all. We all have to ease up on ourselves. No one is perfect and no one expects you to nail every single goal or dream you have.

What do you want to achieve financially?

____

____

____

____

____

____

____

____

____

____

I am so proud of you. These topics are not easy. I still struggle with each of them from time to time so don't think that just because you map out goals it's always going to be smooth sailing. What matters is that you create the goal. Even more important is that you enjoy the journey along the way as you begin to implement the plans that will lead to reaching your goal.

LET'S TALK PRIORITIES

As you begin to focus on what you want personally, professionally, physically and financially—all the things your girl needs and knows how to achieve—you must address the most important thing to making it all work: Priorities.

Each of us has our priorities. For me, it's my faith, family, health and career—pretty much in that order. I realize that if I am not spiritually sound I am worthless. My family is why I live and what makes me get up in the morning. Just like you, I can't survive without good health, and quite honestly, when it comes to finances, it's much more comfortable to have money than not.

The reason I have been successful thus far is because I have set goals that are in line with my priorities and I have done a good job of keeping those priorities in order. A perfect example is in my current business. Although physically I could go out and speak at conferences five or six times a month, if not more, I won't do it. My maximum is two speaking engagements a month. I could make a lot more money, but my priority is Noah, Paris and David. The time I have with them is more meaningful to me than the money I could make presenting another seminar. When my two dates are booked, all other seminars are conducted by another speaker in my company. I will share lots of systems such as these in future chapters. What I want you to focus on now is what your priorities are and what order they are in.

THINK LIKE THIS GIRL

Many people have priorities in life. The problem is they don't live by them. While they say that faith, family and career are important, and in that order, they end up giving everything they have to their careers, at the cost of losing their families and being spiritually defunct. You must set your priorities and then live by them at all costs.

What are your life's priorities?

1. ______________________________

____

____

2. ______________________________

____

____

3. ______________________________

____

____

4. ______________________________

____

____

5. ____

____

____

6. ____

____

____

PRIORITIES: LIVE BY THEM

Use your priorities as a guide when setting goals. This will allow you to create and live a life that is far beyond anything you could ever imagine for yourself. You will wake up at night and pinch yourself just to make sure that your life is for real. Do not allow any form of limitations to seize your life. Take a big, deep breath, let it out and know that you are on your way to being the woman God meant you to be. The girl you were yesterday is meeting the woman you are today, and these two are becoming a powerful force that people will admire, respect and aspire to be like. Most importantly, this woman is someone you'll love.

FOCUS LIKE THIS GIRL:

Chapter Summary

1. Others will tell you to be cautious, not to set your sights too high for fear of being let down, or that you already have more than you need. This is not true. Throw caution to the wind, go for your dreams and make them big.

2. Who cares if you fail? You can get back up and try again. Yes, you may have what you need. But do you have what you want?

3. As women, we have been brainwashed to believe that our sole purpose is to serve others. While this may be a big part of your life and something you are proud to do, you must also serve yourself. You matter.

4. Goals are targets. You can't hit the bull's eye if you don't know where it is. The same holds true with your life. To accomplish the goals and dreams you desire, you must first know what they are. The first step is to write your goals down and own them.

5. To achieve balance and peace of mind, you must set goals according to your priorities. Stay true to yourself and what matters most while pursuing those goals that can have a tremendous impact on your life.

SECTION II

Build Life-Changing Systems

chapter five

Grow

LET'S TALK SPIRITUAL, PHYSICAL AND MENTAL GIRL POWER

If I were driving from Florida to New York, before I put the key in the ignition, I would make sure I had a map. No one in her right mind would take a road trip without some sort of directions in hand. At one time we had to get a big map from AAA, unfold it across the front seat, and follow the route highlighted. Perhaps you remember those days. Today we are blessed with incredible technology that allows us to simply program an address into the GPS. Not only do we have directions, but a personal travel attendant. Should we get lost the attendant politely suggests alternate routes. It doesn't get much easier than this.

Whether planning a road trip or something as complex as your life, following directions is half the battle. When people ask me how I published my first book, I often say, "I followed the directions." I literally bought *The Idiots Guide to Getting Published* and did exactly what the author said to do. I then supplemented that first how-to book with *The Guide to Literary Agents* and began seeking an agent, starting with the letter A. I committed to writing every agent in the

United States through the letter Z, until I was accepted and published. While many aspiring authors choose to believe they won't ever get published, I chose to believe that all I needed was one agent. If just one agent liked my work, my efforts would be a success. In truth, the odds were in my favor. There were thousands of agents. Wouldn't just one find what I had to say of interest? Instead of seeing the 2,999 who wouldn't like my work, I put the focus on the one agent who would.

> THINK LIKE THIS GIRL
>
> *To change your life you must change your thoughts. Put your focus on what you want. You can go through life with a map that provides clear directions and focuses on where you're trying to go, or you can wing it and cross your fingers in hope that you'll somehow magically get there.*

In everything you do, in each aspect of your life, put focus on the result you want. When negative thoughts and fears creep in, acknowledge that they are there and purposefully restate them to give energy to what you want. Flip the negative to a positive, I mean. Your job, with the help of this book, is to focus on creating the girl and life you want. *Get Your Girl Back* is the map.

We have explored who you were, who you are right now, and who you want to be tomorrow. Now it's time to educate yourself about the day-to-day tools you'll need to get your girl back. Let's start with the most important priority in your life right now: You. This chapter will focus on your spiritual, physical and mental well-being. You are going to learn what no one ever taught you: How to make yourself a priority and not feel guilty doing it.

MAKE YOURSELF A PRIORITY

Ten years ago this July 4th, we buried my beautiful mother-in-law, Patricia Mary Bild. No one ever imagined she would not be here to see her grandchildren born, her daughter married, her son graduate law school, or that she would be unable to spend her retirement living in the beautiful Gulf-front home she and my father-in-law built together. Pat was always there for us. She had this amazing Woody

HOW *THIS* GIRL DOES IT: *CARY SHERK*

When I was five, I lost my older sister Deborah to leukemia. I remember feeling alone and scared and really afraid of something happening to my parents. When I was 13, I felt there was more to life, and I wanted to give my life to Jesus. I felt a real peace in my heart for the first time. I remember journaling and praying to God everything that I was feeling.

I was so proud of myself that I dared to go away to college, but I was still searching and looking for that girl. I didn't make a lot of friends in college, because I was afraid of opening up, then having them leave. I ended up with a social work degree. My career with the ACTS Retirement Life Community was the beginning of getting my girl back. Recently a client, Grace, helped me to find greater peace. "If you know Jesus," she said, "and if you know you are going to be with Him in heaven when you die, what are you afraid of?"

In the past five months, I've grown in ways I could never have imagined. I've been exercising and have lost 10 pounds. I ran my first 5K, in honor of my sister Deborah. I'm starting to rekindle and develop lasting female friendships. I'm scheduling "Cary time" for the first time in my life. I get regular massages and work out four or five days a week. I'm working on getting rid of my anxiety and fear, and being less worried about what people think. Because of my sister's death, I felt so lost. I never really felt like I had my girl. But now, with my faith and the work to get my girl back, I feel like I'm getting her back again.

Woodpecker laugh and was always cooking up a storm in the kitchen. I'll never forget her showing me how to properly plant flowers or cut a perfect pear. She was a true matriarch.

She left some great memories. But sadly, what I recall most often is our fears surrounding her breast cancer. When we first found out that her cancer was stage four, we went to the temple, as my husband's family is Jewish, and said a prayer with the Rabbi in front of the bema. A very strong family, we all stood there with one another: my father-in-law Jeff, Pat, David, and a few other family members. As the Rabbi prayed, I felt my head begin to throb. I had held the tears for so long that they were clamoring to spill out and fill the entire temple. No one else was crying so I stood firm. Suddenly, my eyes met Pat's and the dam broke. We ran into each other's arms and cried like little children. I felt her fear and prayed with all my heart that a miracle would save her life.

Today, each time I enter the temple, I shed a tear, though it's been ten years. I always think of Pat when I look at the beautiful stained glass windows she helped design for the sanctuary. She was an amazing artist, mother, friend, wife and human being. Yet the truth is, she never made herself a priority. Always consumed by what was happening in the family, she went several years without a mammogram. Even when she felt the lump, she waited. That lump grew and consumed her life and our lives. Cancer spread from the breast to the brain and into all of our lives, stealing the years my mother-in-law should have had with us. Pat will never meet my children, at least not in this realm.

If only. How many times have you said that? I have said it a lot. Unfortunately when you're saying that, it's too late. As a woman, you have to put yourself on the list. I bet you write down everything that needs to be done for the day, from grocery shopping to carpooling to paying bills to making calls to returning emails to grooming the dog. But how often do you put yourself on the list? At the end of the day, is there anything that is simply for you? Things like:

- Schedule a mammogram
- Go for a walk
- Read a nice book or magazine article
- Call a friend and catch up
- Lie down for a rest

How *This* Girl Does It: Michele Leach

I never really felt that I had a strong foundation with religion growing up. My religious background was very spotty. My father would not go to church, and my mother did her best to take us to the church she felt most connected to at the time. For a year we went to the Baptist church; another year the Presbyterian church; another, the Methodist church; another, not at all. Looking back I imagine she might have been on her own spiritual journey.

My husband came from a strong Catholic family. They attended Mass every week. I was always very spiritual and knew that God exists. I never really felt like I had to practice it. After the birth of my first daughter, I began thinking, "Is my family going to become Catholic?" I knew that I wanted my children to grow up with a foundation that they can rely on when things are hard.

The past few years I have begun to question organized religion. There is an empathetic and compassionate side to my personality that is emerging. There's something magical inside of me. For me, it all comes down to being a loving and giving person, and I'm not changing in a way that's going to hurt anyone. It's all a good thing.

Every day I look around and wonder, "How could you not believe in God?" because life is beautiful, and you have to see it. I try to wake up every day and realize how much I'm thankful for.

Imagine how good it would feel to just have one item on your daily list that is for you. Even more importantly, imagine how good it would feel if you made it onto the list and completed the task. Pat never put herself on the list. I am certain, had she known the end result, things would have been different. Allow me to speak up for your children, friends, spouse, parents, and anyone else who loves you. Put yourself on the list every single day. While difficult to do at first, it will get easier and easier.

> THINK LIKE THIS GIRL
>
> *If God wanted you to be a superhero he would have given you a cape.*

Today is a new day. You are going to live your life in color and with purpose. In all my travels over the past 20 years, I have found that the one thing women want more than anything is to be happy. This word is so overused that many people don't even know what it means anymore. Yet still there's this deep, deep hunger for something more.

YOUR SPIRITUAL WELL-BEING

I must be insane to take on this topic but I'll give it a whirl. While I would rather leave this section out entirely, I know without a doubt that spiritual confusion is what holds many readers back from finding their girls. I am no theologian. I am simply a woman who has been on a spiritual journey my entire life and who has had the opportunity to meet thousands of other women who are also on a spiritual journey. What I do know is that if you are spiritually empty you will never be happy and you will never get your girl back.

I grew up a Christian in every sense of the word. While my mom did not take my brothers and me to church, she talked about God regularly and instilled a strong sense of faith in us. From the time I was a child, God had his hand on my life. I often found myself tagging along to church with anyone who would take me. It didn't matter whether the church was Methodist, Lutheran, or Baptist. I just wanted to be close to God. Before long I realized that God was not only in church, he (or she) was everywhere. I have been to churches that have been life-changing and I have been to churches that have been destructive. At 42, I get why people are so confused and messed up over religion. We rely on other humans to help us interpret the Bible and the place of God in our lives. Think about it. Each person has his or her own opinion and beliefs. Similarly, each church has its own ideas.

When you have children and begin to share your spiritual or religious beliefs, you begin to ask yourself, "Is this even possible?" While others won't say it out loud, I will: Religion is downright complicated. Why did it take me over 30 years to fully understand the trinity when I've been a believer my whole life? Should I expect it to take my children that long?

My goal is not to confuse you further, but to create an open dialogue. The goal is for you to be honest with yourself about where you are in your spiritual journey. I'll share my truths if you share yours. The only caveat is that neither of us gets to judge the other. I believe God made us curious creatures and that it's normal to ask lots of difficult questions. Many religions expect you to just accept what you are told and carry on. That doesn't work for me. I can't wait to sit next to God and talk about life and get the answers to the many questions I have. To get your girl back, you must make peace with your religion or find a new one that brings you peace.

A MEMORABLE MOMENT

I will never forget one of my first dates with Dave, back in college. We were at Hooters when out of the blue he said, "I'm Jewish." For a moment, I couldn't even speak. *What?* I thought. I had known only one Jew in my life. I was stumped. This was the last thing I expected to come out of Dave's mouth. We already had an incredible connection, yet with his statement I felt complete despair because I had always been told that one should be equally yoked with her spouse—follow the same religion, in other words. I did everything possible in that first month to end our relationship. Yet day after day I was drawn closer and closer to him. And in my heart, I knew that God's hand was on my life. While the rules of man I'd been taught said our love was wrong, I knew it was right. Twenty-two years later, I can't help but wonder where I would be now, had I trusted what man said versus what God spoke in my heart. Our relationship felt true and real. There was no anguish within me or between me and God, just between me and man's law. I followed my heart.

In the time since, Dave and I have respected each other's beliefs and neither has tried to convert the other. What I have learned is religious tolerance. How can I expect Dave to change everything he knows just to please me? We are a product of our beliefs. How can he expect me to change my beliefs just to please him? Dave and I decided we would learn from each other. I have come to believe that people are more alike than they are different, whether Christian, Jewish, Buddhist or Muslim. We are all doing our very best, depending on our cultures and backgrounds, to seek out and love the God or spirit or light or path we have been introduced to.

> THINK LIKE THIS GIRL
>
> *Ninety-nine percent of what each religion believes is the same. Sadly, it's the 1% difference that has cost millions upon millions of people their lives. —David Bild*

On my journey to get my girl back, I put the issue of religious differences to bed once and for all. I decided that God and his love, not man and his hate, would win in my marriage. God is love. I was not going to let the religious wars that have plagued our world for generations come into my home. I chose love. Once I did that—and let go of the guilt, shame and concern over what other people thought—I found complete spiritual peace in my life and in my marriage. To this day, Dave and I grow ever closer and have a greater understanding of each other's faith because of our commitment to find spiritual peace and to protect our marriage.

Whatever your religion or faith, you must seek complete peace to get your girl back. Know that God loves you and wants you to have the most amazing life possible. Even better, he will help you get it.

THINK LIKE THIS GIRL

God has more planned for you than you can ever imagine for yourself.

What is holding you back right now from experiencing spiritual peace?

____

____

____

____

____

What religious shame or guilt do you carry?

Who can you talk to who will help you to begin to find peace? This must be someone trustworthy, who will listen with an open heart and mind.

How will you arrange to speak with this person? Make a plan and write it here.

Okay, you've done a lot of work! Now it's time to sit and reflect. In your own words, what is your overall spiritual goal?

My example: My goal is to continue the system I set up (below), keep an open mind to religious differences, and make God the center of my life every day.

Your turn now!

____

____

____

____

To find your own personal spiritual well-being, you must have a system in place that allows you to consistently nurture your spirit. If you don't, you will live on a spiritual rollercoaster: up and strong one day, low and a wreck the next. Underlying your goal must be the desire to achieve a sense of peace that lives within you every single day. Since we get what we focus on, that means you must focus on bringing spiritual peace into your life. What you must figure out is what works for you.

To me, God is love. God loves you more than you can imagine and wants you to feel peace and happiness. To get your girl back, you must find the path to spiritual peace and own it. Below, I have outlined the system I use. It's your turn next, so use my ideas to inspire your own:

1. I pray daily, all throughout the day. In my life, God is everywhere.

2. I read daily journals, reflect on my dream books every week and reread what I wrote while sitting on my porch watching the sunset. I prepare a cappuccino, read, and simply contemplate life.

3. I keep my kids involved in church and support my church financially (although I will admit, I don't go often. I love knowing that should I need the guidance of my pastor or church, both are there for me).

4. I trust God in all matters of my life. As my mother always taught me: If it feels right, it is and if it doesn't, it's not.

I think that each day, a person should take time for some sort of meditation or prayer. Whatever your faith, seek it out and attempt to better understand it. Focus on what your spirit needs. You will know when you find it because it will feel incredibly good. You will feel lighter in everything you do, be happy, and content. Read books, purchase devotionals, or perhaps talk to spiritual mentors. The things you need to bring peace into your life will reveal themselves to you. Most importantly, trust your intuition. If something feels right keep moving in that direction. God lives in you and will speak if you will only listen.

What action steps can you take for yourself on a daily basis that will move you toward finding spiritual peace and balance?

1. ______________________________

   ____

2. ______________________________

   ____

3. ____

____

4. ____

____

Now be aware that parents, siblings and others may challenge you to do what they want you to do versus what you feel you need to do. So it's really important to think ahead and come up with what you'll say if they challenge you. Use "I" messages, as in, "I need to do this to feel better about myself." They are more powerful and sound less defensive and argumentative than "you" messages, as in, "You just wouldn't understand how I feel."

____

____

____

____

____

____

____

____

PHYSICAL WELL-BEING

As you seek spiritual peace, also begin to seek out those things that will bring you peace with your body. Before I found my girl, peace to me would have been to lose weight. Having invested time to better understand myself and my body, I now know that physical peace involves not only looking good, but feeling good—feeling vibrant and alive, with tons of stamina and patience, and as few illnesses as I can manage to control. What I care about isn't just how my body looks, but how it performs.

Okay, now you take a moment and think about your body. What do you want for your body? How do you want to feel and look? Please don't get discouraged, just have fun and dream.

____

____

____

____

____

Based on this, what would you say is your most important goal when it comes to overall physical peace or health?

My example: My goal is to maintain a size 6 jeans, eat water-based, live foods, have lots of energy, and sleep well at night.

Now it's your turn:

____

____

____

____

____

Good job! Okay, now, what action steps can you take daily to reach your goal?

Example: My action steps:

1. Exercise three times a week, no exceptions.

2. Eat lots of fish, vegetables and superfoods daily. Pre-plan meals and snacks for the week.

3. Drink water throughout the day, maintain a stress-free environment, and breathe.

Now your turn. (It's okay if you only want to commit to one to get you started. Big changes come from small beginnings.)

1. ______________________________

____

2. ______________________________

____

3. ______________________________

____

How does it feel to get in the driver's seat and take control? No more excuses, right? Just as a car will break down if not cared for, so will your body. Pay attention to how your body feels and respond to it by giving it what it needs.

MENTAL WELL-BEING

One of the most difficult tasks to getting your girl back is finding and maintaining mental well-being. Yet in truth, once mastered, it becomes the easiest. The secret? You must maintain control of your thoughts. You are what you think. Mental well-being is a choice but it also requires tremendous discipline. Our minds are pre-programmed to think negatively. To think positively requires work. In short, you must retrain your brain.

Like you, I have to work at this. It helps to be proactive. I do things daily to fuel my brain and prevent negativity from taking hold. I find mental peace in the most unexpected places. Often it's the simple things.

» Going to Starbucks, grabbing a latte, and reading a good book while listening to soft music and taking in the aroma of coffee.

» Strolling a bookstore and flipping through books on cooking, parenting and gardening.

» Taking a long walk along a nature trail while listening to my favorite music.

» Having a long, intimate talk with my husband, David.

» Going out on my bedroom balcony and watching as God paints the sunset.

» Weeding my garden.

» Grabbing Paris or Noah and wrapping my arms around them so tight that I fear they will break.

What kinds of things allow your mind to take a break?

____

____

____

____

____

____

____

In the space below, write down your mental goal.

My example: To control my mind, have mental clarity, and use it as a tool to positively impact my life.

Your turn:

____

____

____

____

____

____

What one to three action steps can you take daily that will ensure you reach your desired goal?

My example:

1. Spend time in my garden: Monday, Wednesday and Friday.
2. Take a ten-minute coffee break daily to meditate and breathe.
3. Give thanks and gratitude each day, throughout the day, for the blessings I have.

Okay, now it's your turn:

1. ____

____

2. ____

____

3. ____

____

When you give attention to your well-being—spiritual, physical and mental—you help to create it. To get what you want, you have to know what you want and clearly define it.

COMMIT

Find a piece of paper or poster board and write down your spiritual, physical and mental goals and action steps. Put this document where you can see it every single day. You might tape it to your computer, your bathroom mirror or your car's dashboard.

Writing down your action steps is not enough. You also must give them life by reading them over and over. That's how you start retraining your brain. Each time you look at your list you will become more powerful. While the first week you might read an action plan item and laugh out loud because you did not do it, the next week your mind will be working overtime in an attempt to help ensure you do that very task. Remember, the mind wants a job and in this case you are telling it exactly what to do. You are in control of your life and your life will get on track and find the course you have programmed it to take.

I am so proud of you. You have done a lot of work. This journey will begin with you at the top of the list so that you have the power and strength needed to impact the lives of those you love and support each and every day. No fear, no guilt, just pure power. Your girl is coming back. I can see her and she is more powerful than you could ever imagine.

GROW LIKE THIS GIRL:
Chapter Summary

1. Perhaps for the first time in your life, *you* are going on the priority list. While this may seem difficult at first and guilt will try to detract you, stay focused. The greater balance you have, the more you are able to help those you love most. Give yourself permission to actively take care of yourself every day and see the impact this decision has on every aspect of your life.

2. In everything you do, in each aspect of your life, focus on the result you want. When negative thoughts creep in, acknowledge them compassionately, then purposefully flip them into positive thoughts. That's how you'll get the energy and guidance to achieve your goals.

3. Put yourself on the "to do" list every day and make it a point to complete the tasks you listed. Make yourself a priority.

4. Whatever your religion or faith, seek spiritual peace. Don't rely on others to tell you what to believe. Look for your own answers.

5. Each day, make time for some sort of meditation or prayer. Whatever your faith, attempt to better understand it. Focus on what your spirit needs. You will know when you find it because it will feel incredibly good.

6. Look in the mirror and see what's good.

GROW LIKE THIS GIRL:

Chapter Summary

(Continued)

7. You are what you think you are. Mental well-being is a choice but it also requires tremendous discipline.

8. By giving focus and attention to your spiritual, physical and mental well-being, you will begin to attract it.

chapter six

LOVE

LET'S TALK RELATIONSHIPS AND MARRIAGE!

The word relationship covers a lot of ground and since this is girl talk, I'm going to get right to the point and discuss the relationship with your significant other first. We will get to the kids, family and friends in subsequent chapters. First things first: your mate (or dream mate). As much as you might act like you don't need or want a partner in life, most women, when it comes down to it, do. This is nothing to be ashamed of. It's our nature. In fact, no matter how much success, fame, or money you have, none of it matters if there is no one to share it with. It is innate to love and be loved.

Let's start by talking about existing relationships. If you just got out of one, this chapter might help you better understand what went wrong and what you might do differently next time to ensure your relationship is built to last. I value the sanctity of marriage and while others mock that belief and say it's not necessary, I believe it is. We must be able to commit to one another for the long haul, not just when it's easy and comfortable. Most of us said the words, "For better or worse, for richer or for poorer, and in sickness and in health."

What about, "Through sleep deprivation, dirty diapers, financial strain, weight gain, decreased sex drive and utter chaos?"

> **THINK LIKE THIS GIRL**
>
> *You have to want the man more than the wedding. While the wedding is temporary, the man is permanent. Don't confuse one for the other.*

How many times have you read a book that ended with the phrase, "And they lived happily ever after"? It wasn't until I had Noah, my son and second child, that I realized the stark contrast between books written for boys and those written for girls. Most of Noah's books talked about simple things such as cars or friendship. My daughter's, on the other hand, typically ended with, "And they lived happily ever after." I quickly began changing the endings to Paris's favorite stories—Snow White, Cinderella, Sleeping Beauty, and others—to, "And they lived happily ever after, *with lots of hard work*."

Let's face it: Women want the fairy tale. Even Kate Middleton, who not too long ago married a real life prince and who had the fairy tale wedding, will quickly find that there is no happily ever after. Yet for a moment, the world, mostly women, was glued to the television, in hopes

How *This* Girl Does It: *Michele Leach*

My husband works so hard and has provided us an amazing life. I get to be who I am because of him. We try to spend time talking, instead of telling. I think that's one of the biggest problems in marriage today. We spend so much time "telling" (where to be, who to pick up, etc.) that we forget to spend time just talking. To me, that's a beautiful thing.

that perhaps this time there could be. Deep down in our cores, we want it for Kate and Wills, because that means it's possible for us too.

I vividly remember being a young girl and fantasizing about my prince. The setting was the Old Hickory Grove Road trailer park. I would ride my pink Huffy bike through the streets, wind blowing through my hair, and dream of my prince. I was seven or eight, had wispy blond hair, milk chocolate eyes and jet black eyebrows. I would park my bike and hold court with my friends, sharing the stories of how I came to be in Urbana, Ohio. "I was a princess who came by boat and ended up here due to an accident at sea. My kingdom was far away but the realm knew I was alive and one day they will find me." Then I'd jump back on my bike and conjure up images of my prince who I just knew was waiting for me. I was so full of curious imaginings: *What would he look like, where was he from, and when exactly would I meet him?* I would imagine the many places we would go and think about my happily ever after.

These memories are so real, so fresh that I can almost feel that cool breeze on my face. I was young, innocent and full of dreams. I never questioned for a moment whether my prince would come. When I told my stories they were real and when I dreamed of the future, it was as if it were already written. I owned that trailer court and it is where I first learned to dream and visualize my future.

SOMEDAY MY PRINCE WILL COME

It's bittersweet to peek into the past while immersed in the present. The prince of my dreams is no longer a mystery. He is David Henry Bild. While I was once consumed with who my prince would be, what he'd look like and where he'd come from, I now have all those answers. My prince was to come from Clearwater Florida, have thick, long, blond hair, hazel eyes and a heart of gold. He did not ride in on a horse but instead flew in on an airplane. He did not hail from a royal family but certainly one of good standing. Looking back, I still

How *This* Girl Does It:
Yasmine Sharp

My husband and I dated for seven years. I knew I wanted to marry someone that I was passionately in love with. I wanted someone who would support me and empower me, but not control me. I knew that I was always going to work to keep a spark in my marriage. We remained pure until our wedding. That was really important to me, as a way to honor my very traditional Pakistani parents. I always joke that I have to keep it sexy in the bedroom, because I made my husband wait for seven years. He is the nicest, gentlest, most patient man you will ever meet. He is my number one biggest supporter.

can't believe my good fortune. I did not get a prince, I got a king. I don't know if it was luck, the hand of God, or my vision simply manifested into reality. I accepted the blessing Dave has been in my life and work diligently every day to make sure he stays.

Like me, more than likely, you also have the answers to this very same question. Is the man you envisioned the man you are with today? If we were having lunch and I asked you to tell me about him, what would you say? What if he were eavesdropping and heard you describe him to me, how would he feel? As we discuss the importance of relationships, it is essential that you learn to see the man you are with for who he really is. Just like you have been buried and at times lost in the chaos of life, odds are that he has been too. Think back and ask yourself: What was he like when you first met? Why did you fall in love with him? What qualities drew you to him? Now focus on these traits. Make sure that you take the time and effort to compliment him and remind him why you fell in love with him in the first place and what you appreciate about him today.

Girlfriend, let me be clear. Complimenting your man doesn't come easy. It's easier to pick on him and point out what he hasn't done than it is to stroke his ego and make him proud of what he has done. Be cautious of this because a man needs to feel loved, important and valued. You must make a conscious effort to say what you are thinking. If you come home and find that your husband or significant other has unloaded the dishwasher, make a point of saying "thank you" later in the day. While you unload it every single day and he never says "thank you," it doesn't matter. As women, it's in our nature to be caretakers and to simply get things done. Men are not wired the same. They want to tinker and fix. They are the hunters. When they step into your reality and make a contribution, no matter how small, say thanks. What you will find is your mate will help out more often because you notice. The more you praise him, the more his pride in you and his family will grow. He will feel like the man of the house, the king of his domain, and that is what he was designed to be. The added bonus is that your partner will more than likely start to reciprocate and offer compliments to you.

THINK LIKE THIS GIRL

A compliment doesn't cost a dime. Give it freely and see the impact it makes on your relationship.

EXPECTATIONS

Looking back into your own past, did you ever dream of your one true prince? Did you get him? Is he still in your life, or did he turn into a frog? Whatever your answer, together you and I are going to add to the story or perhaps even rewrite it. The amount of work your story needs depends on how you answer these questions: If you were reading a fairy tale about your own life, would you want to continue reading? Would the man you're with today fulfill the vision you had of your one true prince? Or would you add a few characteristics or traits that are currently missing? Is your story one you'd want to read to your own daughter or niece? If not, this chapter is vitally important to getting your girl back and it will be one of the most challenging chapters yet. For this reason, if you have not yet gone to my website, www.GYGB.com, do so right now and sign up for "Notes From Your Girl" and become a fan of our Facebook page at Get Your Girl Back Movement. I, along with thousands of other women on a journey similar to yours, will offer support, encouragement and advice as you seek to make the changes needed to transform your life.

I was recently reading *Vogue* magazine when I came upon an article written by Shiva Rose, called "The Grimm Truth." She was discussing the end of her fairy tale marriage to a Hollywood actor. As I read the article, I saw a clear example of a young, strong, powerful woman slowly losing her girl and then longing to get her back. Here is an excerpt from her article: "I suppose my 'magic year' was when I was 26. I was in a stable marriage, I had a baby girl, and I was bursting with ambition and hope."

This is a perfect example of the girl I often refer to in this book. Your girl is present at a time in your life you can vividly remember, when you could do anything—a time when you were sure of yourself, confident and in control. Shiva then went on to say: "Nine years later, I became pregnant with our second daughter. This was a more sober journey than the first. As much as I tried to replicate what I had years before, there were changes. My marriage was beginning to fray, and I found myself alone during much of my pregnancy because of my husband's schedule. I had health issues, as did my unborn baby. The only solace I could find was in the mountains of Topanga, where my older daughter was blossoming into an equestrienne."

Those sad words reflect a woman who has lost her girl, in a matter of nine short years. Don't let this happen to you! Or, if it has happened, fix it now! Life is full of unexpected twists and turns. Each one sucks a little bit more out of you. The key is to recognize and know how to get your girl back.

> THINK LIKE THIS GIRL
>
> *If someone is going to have the fairy tale ending, why shouldn't it be you?*

A thought that must be tattooed on your mind by now is, "You get what you focus on." Your current relationship is a direct representation of your thoughts. While you might not want to admit it, it's true. Look at the two examples below and be honest with yourself. Which thought process most represents your daily thought pattern?

EXAMPLE #1:

» My husband never helps with the kids. He comes home from work, turns on the television, and the kids all run and jump in his lap. While I've done all the work, he gets to be the hero. I'm always the bad guy. What gives?

» My husband doesn't do anything around the house. If I don't do it, it doesn't get done.

» I feel like a piece of meat. Doesn't my husband understand I'm tired and don't want to have sex? I've worked, taken care of the kids, and there he is, standing in line. One more person wanting something from me.

What kind of relationship does this thought process create? More than likely it stimulates a stressed out, tense union where there is little support and much discord. There is little in the way of tenderness, complimenting or sincere affection. Odds are both sides are depressed and angry. If this describes your relationship, is this really what you want? If your answer is no, then you must commit to implementing the systems I outline in this chapter. In as little as a month your relationship can be completely reborn.

EXAMPLE #2:

» My husband is a great dad. I know how much he loves our kids and I value the time he gives to them as well as the effort he makes to be a wonderful father.

» My husband does the best he knows how. Let's face it; I'm a bit more particular than he is when it comes to the home yet he pitches in when I ask him to. I have to remember to ask for help when I need it and not expect him to read my mind.

» If I meet my husband's physical needs, I actually feel closer to him. I must make him a priority just as I make my kids a priority.

In contrast to the first example, what kind of relationship does this thought process create? It's safe to say that both people involved are happy and fulfilled in their relationship. They collaborate and support each other in their parenting and feel loved, cared for and respected. Because they are intimate they have a close bond and feel connected to each other in a powerful way. There's lots of hugging, flirting and laughter in this relationship. If this describes you, Girlfriend, then thumbs up! This is a huge accomplishment. No pressure—but whatever you do, don't mess it up!

Relationships change over time. If your answer is example one, it's okay. Trust me, I've been there. While example two might sound like a script from a fairy tale, trust me, it can be your reality a month from now. The sooner you learn to get control of your thoughts and how you perceive and think about your man, the faster you will see that much-needed change.

To improve your marriage or relationship, you first must know what it is you want out of it. Take a moment and assess your marriage.

Describe your current marriage or relationship by finishing these statements.

» Our communication is ______________________________

____

» When we spend time together it's ____________________

____

» When I see him I____________________________________

____

» People who know us say______________________________

____

» When I ponder our future together I__________________

____

What, if anything, would you improve? You are not allowed to pick on your man right now. Look at the marriage or relationship as a whole and ask yourself what you would like to change. Maybe you don't communicate, touch one another, or even know who the other is anymore. Whatever the situation, please know that you have the ability to turn things around and create the relationship you desire. Okay, make your list. Be gentle!

Anything worth having takes work. I imagine that right now, your relationship is at the top of your list and your desire is to get as close to that darn fairy tale as you can. Here's a system that will set you on your way.

SIX SYSTEMS TO TRANSFORM YOUR MARRIAGE OR RELATIONSHIP

1. **Make time for each other.**

One of the most important systems that Dave and I put in place when we had kids was date night. Paris, my older child, just turned nine. Each week, since she was just a few months old, we have had a minimum of one, if not two date nights a week. This commitment to each another is what has kept our marriage rock solid. Some weeks are so busy with the two kids, my business, school, sports activities, Dave's travel schedule, and a dozen other things happening that we barely make eye contact let alone have a full blown conversation. Yet come Wednesday and Saturday, I know that if Dave is not traveling, we are going out or at least spending quality time together at home after the kids are in bed and without the television on. My mom is set up to watch our kids. There are many nights when I'm tired and simply don't want to go out but realize how important it is to our relationship so I do it. Once out, I find myself having fun, relaxing and connecting with Dave in a wonderful way. We don't spend a lot of money on our dates but we do have one rule: Do not get stuck in the dinner and a movie rut. Although dinner and a movie is nice once in awhile, it gets mundane and leads to complacency. Keeping a marriage alive requires thinking out of the box, keeping things interesting and putting forth lots of effort. We both come up with ideas. Sometimes it's a bike ride on a nearby nature trail for a couple hours. Or it might be a game of racquetball, a comedy club, dancing, the pub with friends, and so on. Not allowing ourselves to settle for what's easy forces us to think, and in truth, have more fun. I look forward to our date night because it's the same kind of experience we had when we first met. We have adventure and excitement built into the evening. As I say this, if you only have one date a week, do not include friends. You need time alone with your mate to talk and connect and if you are with other people you cannot do that. The same holds true with vacations. I meet so many people who travel with other couples on every vacation. A whole week can pass and rather than spending time with each another, they spend time with friends and acquaintances and come back the same as when they left. The goal is to grow closer. So go with just the two of you.

Many marriages or relationships die of boredom. While couples work hard during the courting process to enchant one another, once the vows are said and the marriage license signed, it often becomes a mundane routine. Don't believe me? Take a moment and ask yourself these quick, simple questions:

» When was the last time you went on a fun date and did something other than go to dinner and (or) a movie?

» What did you wear on your last date? Is it something you would have worn on one of your first dates?

» When is the last time you gave your husband or significant other a true, sincere compliment? What was it? If you can't remember, it's been too long.

- What do your pajamas look like?
- Do you still wear perfume?
- When is the last time you gave your husband or significant other a card or wrote him a love letter?

These are just a few things to consider. Maybe you feel really good about your answers. Perhaps you feel bad right now and want to slam this book shut. The most important thing you can do to improve your marriage or relationship is take a look at where it is right now and determine where you want it to go in the future and what needs to happen to get it there.

Whoever said that marriage takes work is a genius. I've been married for many years and not a week has gone by that has not required effort on my part. Date night is required! If you don't have family support or the ability to swap sitting with another mom, use the money you would have spent on a date and pay for a sitter. Think about it. You can easily spend $50 at dinner. Take some of this money to pay your sitter and do something that is free on your date instead. Here are some ideas:

- Do something outdoors together such as rollerblading, biking, walking, running or hiking. Exercise increases sex drive, so who knows, you might just get lucky!
- Scour your local paper for free events such as a movie or concert in the park. Go to a museum. Or dream together by looking at model homes, boats or that new car you want someday.

» Try something you've never done. Take turns trying out fun ideas such as go-cart racing, paddle boarding, fishing, etc. Most of these things are very inexpensive and will create adrenaline and fun.

While taking the time to develop your marriage or relationship and really connecting may be difficult at first, it will become the most fulfilling aspect of your time. Take the first steps and start moving forward. The rest will come naturally. Imagine the feeling of being in love with your spouse or significant other again. Think of the impact it will have on your family. If you have children, it's so wonderful for your kids to see you kiss, dance, laugh and play together in a fun way rather than fight, yell, and bite each other's heads off. This is serious stuff, as you are setting an example for your own children about what they should expect from their own relationships. There is so much at stake here, so make the time, starting this week.

2. **Be willing to work hard at the relationship.**

To grow your marriage or relationship and really enjoy it as if you are on a never-ending date, you have to get real and acknowledge that it is going to take work. As much as you love someone, you are two different people with different experiences, opinions and ideas about how things should be done. If you have children, that adds another dimension.

The most difficult time in my marriage occurred after having children. It wasn't the kids that provided the challenge but the differences in religion and how our children would be raised. As I shared in the last chapter, Dave is Jewish and I am Christian. Prior to having kids Dave wasn't concerned about how we would one day raise them spiritually. Once Paris turned five, Dave came to me and said that it was time for her to start religious school. I could not believe what I was hearing. She had been in church since the time she was born and suddenly he wanted to teach her Judaism? Little did I know that "Sunday school" for Jewish children starts in kindergarten.

To put it lightly, I threw a fit. I cried for weeks and found myself in complete turmoil. I talked to a lot of people who had interfaith marriages that ended in divorce over this very issue and I was scared. I simply did not know how to get over it. Dave and I talked to the Rabbi, I counseled with my pastor, and we tried to find common ground. I was so angry inside and, in truth, terrified for my marriage. One day I was lying in Paris's bed crying when Dave lay down next to me, put his arms around me and said, "I love you Traci. I just want the kids to know my heritage." He was so kind and so sincere that I suddenly knew this was not about one of us winning a battle. People have fought for thousands of years over religion, each group trying to prove how right it was over the other. In that moment I made a decision: Religion would not cause war in my home and it certainly would not destroy my marriage. God is love and I chose love, understanding and compassion.

The healing process began immediately. Once I turned my problems over to God, accepted our differences (instead of fighting to win), and began to support Dave, and work through this difficult time, everything changed. Marriage is about compromise. My compromise was to teach my children both faiths and let them make the decision when the time came of the path they would take. As hard as that was, I had to trust that God would handle the rest and He has.

It took close to two years but we continued to find ways to unite and bring our family together on faith issues. Dave and I both knew this was one of those times in our marriage when we didn't just have to work, but put on the boxing gloves and fight! What do you need to fight for in your own marriage or relationship right now? Is there something you can suggest a compromise on? What is the root cause of the problem, and is it really worth the pain it's causing? How would it feel to get past it? Take some time and write down the ideas that just came to mind:

3. **Make fun a must-have.**

Life is short and most people take it way too seriously. Yes, there are times in our lives that are not enjoyable and moments when we must be very serious. Yet rather than moments, people often spend months, if not years, being far too earnest and downright boring. Ask yourself the following questions:

- When was the last time you laughed until you cried?
- What is the last thing you did with your husband or significant other that was really fun?
- If your husband were to describe you to a stranger, would he say you were fun, grumpy, demanding or uptight?
- Would you like to have more fun, laughter and joy in your life on a daily basis?

Living a life of joy is a choice. If you are grumpy because you spend three to four hours a day carpooling kids to and from sports, doing laundry and paying bills, realize that you and no one else created the circumstances in which you live. Perhaps you work eight to ten hours a day, come home only to make dinner, do laundry, wash the dishes, clean up the house and go to bed, only to wake up and do it all again the next day. Sucks, doesn't it? Trust me, I've been there. I realized early on that this was no way to live and made the changes needed to get out of that rut. I want you to decide right now whether fun should be part of your future and whether it's worth fighting for. If so, take a moment and jot down a few things you can do right now, on a daily basis, to make your marriage or relationship more fun.

I'll start with an example to help get your thoughts flowing. We eat dinner as a family at least five nights a week. Rather than throwing dinner on the table, I always light a candle, turn off the television and put on great music. Sometimes I'll grab Dave or one of the kids and dance. These few simple things often turn a regular night into an extraordinary one. When's the last time you did something fun in your own home?

What can you do, starting today, to make your marriage or relationship more fun? Keep it simple!

____

____

____

____

____

____

Don't forget to check out www.GYGB.com and our Facebook page at Get Your Girl Back Movement to see what other people are doing to spice things up in their marriages and relationships and have more fun.

4. Support and encourage each other.

Like it or not, a man must feel important and needed. The primary person who can deliver that feeling is you. Once upon a time men were the income earners while the women stayed home to care for the home and children. There was a sense of pride among men that no one could take from them. Today, women can take care of themselves, the home and the children. How many times have you heard a woman say, "I don't need a man, I can take care of myself." It's true. Women don't need men like they used to. We can have children on our own thanks to artificial insemination, financially provide for ourselves, and literally "rent a husband" when things need to be done around the house that we can't do. Over time, a man's role in the world has been diminished. To have a successful marriage or relationship, it is crucial that you validate your man and make him feel like he is the most important person in your life. He must know that you both want and need him and the only way he will know that is if you tell him. As you begin to communicate through words, letters, emails, texts, or whatever method you choose, he will begin to reciprocate.

I'm confident that, like your man, you also need to know you matter. While my husband often tells me what a great job I do in business, what I really crave to hear is what a great job I do at home. It means more to me than anything to hear him say what a great mother I am or how much he appreciates everything I do to make our home beautiful and happy. While Dave doesn't say it all the time, he does say it from time to time and it means the world to me. Also, I've noticed a pattern. The more gratitude I show him, in my words and actions, the more he shows me. Marriage and relationships are two-way streets. While you can't change your spouse or significant other, you can change yourself and that is where you must start. Be patient, give it time and realize that you're involved in a game of inches. One hour at a time, one day at a time, your relationship will begin to improve.

Take a moment and think about your husband or significant other. Write down what first comes to mind.

What is happening in your man's life that is causing him stress?

____

____

____

____

____

Now list some things you can do to better support him.

____

____

____

____

____

David is a captain for AirTran Airways. His airline recently merged with Southwest Airlines. While he is excited about working with Southwest, he is under tremendous stress as they negotiate seniority and pay. It's a very complex and long process and it has been weighing on him for months. At times I find myself not wanting to ask him about what's happening with the merger because it's so frustrating and it seems the pilot groups can never agree on anything. Yet I try to make sure, despite my discomfort, to ask what is happening so he knows that I care and understand what he is going through. In short, I put his needs first. When you began dating, I imagine you spent hours on the phone listening to your man. Odds are you sympathized and offered meaningful advice. When was the last time you did that? How might it make him feel if you did? Even more frightening, what if someone else were to offer that support in your place?

DOES YOUR HUSBAND NEED ENCOURAGEMENT?

In today's uncertain world, everyone needs strokes. Whether it's encouragement in finding a new job, getting the bills paid in full and on time, getting control of his health, or something entirely different, I am certain that your reassuring words would make a world of difference. Perhaps the first thing you need to do is just set aside some time to ask questions and better understand what your husband is feeling right now. When and if you do this, make sure you listen. Don't turn it into a session about you and what's happening in your life. Make it a habit to encourage your partner at least once a day in some capacity.

How might you encourage your spouse today?

____

____

____

____

____

____

____

5. Share your dreams and goals.

There's a ton of passion and excitement when people start dating. That's one of the first things that hit me when I read over my girl's letters to Dave when our relationship was brand new. Yet as the years go by, the excitement wears off and complacency sets in. One of the most important things you can do is set goals and dream alongside your spouse. Just as you have dreams, so does he. Do you know what they are? Is there someplace else he'd like to live, a dream job he'd like to have, a hobby he'd like to pursue or a car he'd like to own?

Not too long ago, Julie Podewitz, a former business associate, sent me a picture of her husband's dream board, the place where he posts images of what he'd like to have in his life. "In the close to 15 years I'd known Jim, not once had he ever been interested in the whole dream board thing." Yet after five years of seeing her vision and dream boards, he finally decided to make one of his own. He placed a picture of a Mercedes on the board and a goal to fund a shelter project in Sri Lanka. It was so exciting to see her passion for the future infect him and in turn, they found themselves talking and dreaming together. I know from firsthand experience how passion like that can suffuse the relationship. When you dream together you grow together. You will feel alive and full of possibility, just like when you first met.

What dreams do you have that you'd like to confide in your spouse?

____

____

____

____

____

What dreams does he have? If you don't know, make it a point to find out right away and write them here.

Imagine one year from now the impact it would have on your life and family if you were to partner with your spouse to write your goals, create a vision board, then work as a team toward accomplishing them. Both of you would feel empowered and connected—and your children (if you have them) would see the strength of a united parental front. Rather than each of you working on your own goal, you would be working together toward common goals. One of the reasons Dave and I work so well together is because we are a team. We always have each other's back. It makes a world of difference in your relationship when you know that you have support. Make this a reality in your own relationship. Like it or not, it starts with you. Who else? You're the only one you can control or influence, right?

6. Commit to each other.

Many people enter relationships and even marriages with an exit plan in mind. While a relationship is designed to allow an out, a marriage is not. A perfect example is a prenuptial agreement. While

I do believe they're valid in certain situations, it's also a fact that with a prenup, both parties know there's an easier out should they find something about the relationship not to their liking. Because less pain or discomfort is involved, people call it quits sooner than if there were more discomfort. If you are in a relationship and considering marriage, and your partner asks you to sign a prenuptial agreement, you might want to think twice.

I am only 42 and I have no idea what my future holds. I would like to think my marriage will stand the test of time but I don't have a crystal ball. What I do know is that while I am married, divorce is not an option. What I mean by "commit to each other" is "don't even put divorce on the table." Never, ever use it as a threat in an argument. Sell yourself on the idea that you are in it for the long haul and that no matter what happens, you will find a way to work it out. Look at what you have created together. Why would you want to walk away and start over? In the end, whatever problems you're having in your current marriage, you're more than likely going to have in the next.

Think of the common things that anger you and cause fights in your marriage:

» Your partner is not helping around the house.

» You fight over how to pay the bills or allocate your income.

» Sex—it's never enough.

» Not supporting one another when disciplining the children.

I imagine you can add a lot more to this list. No matter who you are with, these same issues are going to arise. Why start over with someone else rather than work it out with the one you're with? Divorce, in particular, creates incredible pain for everyone involved. If you are not yet married, please take your time and make sure you are ready to commit before heading to the altar. If you are in a marriage now, whether the first, second or third (or more), apply the many principles I have taught you in this book and really commit to a lifetime with your spouse. Be grateful you found the right one for you and make it work. When problems arise, work to find solutions, not an out. You can do it and the payoff will be well worth every ounce of effort.

> THINK LIKE THIS GIRL
>
> *Take the time to figure out what you want out of your relationship. Never, ever settle. Decide what it is you want, not what you can get, and write it down. Once you have done that, determine the action steps that will help move you toward accomplishing your goals.*

In the last chapter, I discussed the importance of setting goals according to your priorities. If you are married or in a relationship, I'm pretty sure that your mate is at the top of your priority list. Take a moment and write your relationship goal. What would you like to see happen there? Remember, you get what you put your focus on. Just as you set your career and life goals, you need goals where your significant other is concerned. I'll start, to get you thinking. Here is my relationship goal for my marriage: To keep my marriage exciting and fun, a lifetime honeymoon.

While this might sound like a strange goal to some, to me, it's everything. When I think of what I want from my marriage, it's just that. I don't want the honeymoon to end, ever. Dave and I have been together for over 20 years. So far, it's been exciting, fun and a lifetime honeymoon. Is it coincidence? No, it's the result of making him a top priority in my life and then making decisions that support that priority. If I want it to last I have to stay on course and do everything possible to support him and the marriage.

What is your relationship goal?

____

____

____

____

Just as you did for your spiritual, physical and mental well-being goals, define specific action steps that will lead you to the achievement of your goal. I'll share mine and then you write yours.

Here are my action steps:

1. Date night once a week
2. Communicate like crazy
3. Laugh together often
4. Annual or mini-vacations

You decide what works for you. Don't overthink things. Ask yourself, what actions will make my relationship goal real if I do them consistently over time? Ideally, you should have three to four.

What actions can you take to support your relationship goal?

____

____

____

____

____

The final step is to post your goal, followed by the action steps, where you can see them every day.

A few words about progressing at your own pace: As you work to get your girl back, you are learning to live your life according to what matters most. You will have clearly defined goals with a plan of action that ensures that you get what you want. That girl of the past is on the path to meet the woman you are today. Don't let her down. You are growing stronger every day and I am so proud of you for getting this far. Remember, getting your girl back is a game of inches, and nothing worth having happens overnight. If it takes you a year or three years to work through this book, take your time. You are crafting the most important work of art you will ever design—your life.

LOVE LIKE THIS GIRL:

Chapter Summary

1. A relationship requires an investment of time. Go into your calendar right now and make some room!

2. Accept that a marriage takes work. Just as a garden will die if you don't water or fertilize it, so will your relationship. You have to tend to it and work to make it beautiful.

3. Your relationship should be fun. Build fun into everyday things, whether dinner, dates, hobbies, or something as something as simple as great music you can dance to or sing along together in the car.

4. Commit to having more fun.

5. You need to support and encourage one another. What people want more than anything is to know that they matter. If you are married, your spouse loved you so much that he pledged his life to you. Make him feel important, needed, understood and as though nothing matters more in your life. In no time at all he will start to do the same for you.

6. The best tactic I know to get closer to your partner is to expose your innermost dreams. Take the time to learn what your man dreams of and share your own. Set goals as a family and celebrate as you accomplish them.

7. Make a point of honoring your vows if you are married. Give 100% to your marriage and commit to a lifetime together. Never use the threat of divorce as a tool to hurt or threaten your spouse.

chapter seven

EMBRACE

LET'S TALK PARENTHOOD AND HOME

Children are proof of God's love for us. Can you imagine any greater gift? There's nothing like it! To those of us who have children, there is nothing more meaningful than being a parent. And there is also nothing more challenging! I'll never forget the night I had a complete and total meltdown, the worst of my relationship with Dave. Paris was two and Noah just six months old. As much as I loved Noah, his inability to sleep through the night took its toll on me. I thought I had communicated to Dave that I needed help but either I was not talking clearly or he did not hear me. Around midnight one night, with both kids in bed, I started screaming at Dave that I needed his help. I was no longer able to get up two times during the night to nurse Noah, plus clean the house, do the laundry, take care of Paris, cook, and run my business. I lost control and took the television remote and threw it square at his head. Barefoot and crazy, I headed out the door, walked to my mom's a few blocks away and cried my heart out to her. I just couldn't do it anymore.

Around three in the morning my mom told me I needed to go home. Dave had been calling all night and I had been refusing to talk to him. I was not going back. I was done. The next morning, she said, "Traci, I think you should go home now. I'm afraid Dave's going to take the kids and leave. He's really upset." That scared me and I went home. Five years later, I could put the whole evening in perspective. I was a crazy, sleep-deprived mother whose hormones were raging. My husband was a wonderful father and incredible helper. He had asked repeatedly if he could give Noah a bottle when he woke up so I could sleep. Up to this point I refused. I, like a lot of mothers, refused to accept help. I had to do it all.

My wiser self now looks back and says, "Girl, what were you thinking?" The next night, Dave and I sat down, talked it out, and decided he would do all feedings between midnight and five am when he was home. He would cook more meals and help around the house. I just had to let him know what I needed. Meaning, I had to tell him because he was not a mind reader. Once we put this new

How *This* Girl Does It: *Diane Weber*

The best time of my life was college. The only responsibility I had was to decide whether or not to put on a baseball cap and sprint to the other end of campus for my 8 am class. That was an awfully early time back then, and a serious sacrifice. Now, by 8 o'clock I've accomplished nothing short of a small miracle by getting three children ready for school. Often, as I sip my cold coffee, unload the dishwasher, throw in a load of laundry, and wonder what's for dinner, I flash back to the girl of my 20s, and wonder, "where did she go?"

After starting to get my girl back, I feel as if I have woken up from the hazy dream that had become my life as a wife and mother. For the first time in my life, I'm actually thinking about getting out of my head and into my mind.

I realize that my mama was right. Everything happens for a reason. My reason for being is to encourage others on this journey called life, and my experiences will be tools for that.

system in place, my life drastically improved. I got sleep, which made me calmer and happier. I got more help day in and day out because I learned to ask.

As women, we have been raised to believe that we have to do it all ourselves. But it is impossible for a woman to do it all on her own and maintain a sense of balance and happiness. The best thing you can do as a woman is to have a strong support system. Yet what do you do if you don't have someone to share in the duties? What if you're single, or you live far away from your family?

As mothers, we want the best for our children. We want to give them every experience we never had, protect them, and send them out into the world to make a difference. I admit that I am no authority on parenthood but this book would not be complete without this chapter because most readers have children. More importantly, most people reading this book lost their girl at least in part as a result of having children. While the sacrifice is worth it, who says you can't enjoy being a mother *and* be your best self by getting your girl back? The goal of this chapter is to address the day-to-day challenges of being a parent and to provide you with systems that will make the tougher part of your job just a little bit easier. Let's be honest. If motherhood simply involved

How *This* Girl Does It: *Michele Leach*

My main dream right now for my children is to have a beautiful childhood. I want them to have an existence where everyday life is good for them. I want them to have a good time and have fun and have a family that supports what they like to do. I'm raising my kids completely different from the way my parents raised me, and I'm okay with that.

I want my household to be peaceful and calm. I don't yell a lot. I want it to be a Zen-like environment when we're here. Friends are surprised when I tell them that my three dogs bring peace and joy to our family.

being with our children, hugging, kissing, talking, playing, advising and loving them, we would keep having more and more and more until our bodies gave out. Being a parent takes a lot of work and is a ton of responsibility. If you don't have kids, you can skip this chapter (but you might find some great home management skills if you stay with me). What I want to address is the crap that gets in the way of your enjoying motherhood:

» Cooking

» Cleaning

» Laundry

» Scheduling

» Discipline

JOIN OUR TEAM

Sounds like a fun topic, doesn't it? When Dave and I moved into our first home, we had been married four years and didn't yet have children. Our new neighbors immediately started talking to us about having kids and how wonderful that would be. As Dave pointed out, they wanted us to join "their team." The parenthood team, that is. When you are dating, all the married people say, "When are you getting married?" It's a subtle, "Come on, join our team." When you're married, it becomes, "When are you going to have kids? Join our team!" You will notice no one ever says, "Oh, by the way, these are the side effects":

» Your body will become a food mill and you will do things you swore you never would do, such as nursing your baby in front of a crowd of strangers just to get her to stop crying.

- » Once said child starts eating real food, you will be responsible for cooking three meals a day, not to mention meal planning, grocery shopping and cleanup for those three squares.
- » Laundry will become your nemesis. No matter how hard you try, there will always be more laundry. A friend of mine has a sign over her laundry room door that says, "Purgatory."
- » You will fret over how smart your kid is and whether she is in the right school, has the right teacher, is being bullied and has the right friends. This will go on for 12 years, not including preschool.
- » You will be in pure anguish, as if your arm were being severed, each time you have to drop your kids off to go to work. Never in your life did you think something could be so emotionally draining.
- » While you promised yourself you would not become your parents, you look in the mirror and say, "Welcome, Mother! So glad you could join me," because she is there, every moment of every day rearing your children through you.

A once spontaneous life becomes strictly predictable because a child without structure becomes a little monster. While I would have for sure had my children under any and all circumstances, and I'm sure you would too, let's be clear: The side effects of motherhood took what was left of your girl. With each increased responsibility and role you took on to be the world's best mom, your girl got buried deeper and deeper. The beautiful hair that everyone complimented you on was pulled into a ponytail; the stylish outfits were replaced by "comfortable" clothes; the stilettos hijacked by flats. Your diva gave way to motherhood and while you always said it was temporary, odds are she never found her way back. If you are like me, she was buried deep inside, anxiously awaiting her return to glory. You know what I'm talking about because from time to time you'd see her. A night on the town as you put on a pair of heels, a cute black dress, sexy red lipstick and *boom*—there she is, only to turn into a pumpkin at midnight because no matter how glamorous you look, you never have enough sleep.

Whether your kids are infants, toddlers or teenagers, you are going to slowly bring your girl back and master the art of kick-ass home economics in this chapter so you can get the necessary stuff done as quickly and efficiently as possible and move on to those things you *want* to do. To make this happen, Girlfriend, you need great systems.

Write down those challenges that are most pressing on you as a mother. If finances come to mind, please hang tight as we are going to address that in the next chapter. You can put anything from spending enough quality time with your children, to dealing with health problems and special needs, to sibling fights to grades.

What are your greatest challenges as a mother right now?

____

____

____

____

____

____

____

Okay, let's get started reducing the mom workload to make time for your girl to come back! It's about survival!

> THINK LIKE THIS GIRL
>
> *Daily systems will transform your life. Implement one new system a month and in less than a year, you will run your life versus having it run over you.*

CREATE A CAPTURE TOOL

People become victims of their own circumstances. Conversely, success is preparation meeting opportunity. If you want to wake up and have a great day, the best advantage you have is knowing what's supposed to happen before it does. This isn't to say there won't be surprises but a little effort will go a long way to minimizing their effects. When I first had my daughter, Paris, I hired a personal coach to help me better manage being a mother and to continue the success of my business despite the added responsibility. One of the most valuable lessons she taught me was to create a capture tool. It's a way to have your calendar, to-do list and important papers all in one place. A capture tool goes where you go. It's like a personal assistant. This is preparation meeting opportunity. You are in control and have the ability to make better decisions as the day or week progresses. Here's how it works.

YOUR CAPTURE TOOL

- **Plan the week:** Each Friday, take a moment to synch calendars—yours, the family's, your husband's, the kids'—for the upcoming week. Incorporate everyone's activities into your master, in other words. I cannot begin to tell you how powerful it feels to get in control of your life. More importantly you will see, in advance, how crazy your life is and why you cannot possibly cram one more thing in. This process allows you to be realistic about your time and to make tough decisions about what needs to come off the calendar to better match up with your priorities. Once you have organized your master calendar, print out each day individually and put them in order, Monday through Sunday, on your clipboard or on your specific capture tool.

• **Review the upcoming week:** Once you print your calendar, be sure to actually look at each day and highlight or circle events you cannot miss. Add notes and get your head around everything coming up. If you don't want to use a clipboard, make sure your cell phone calendar is organized and reviewed each day for the upcoming week. I use the clipboard because I notice that there are lots of important papers parents get from the kids' schools and at sporting events. The clipboard allows me to have a safe place to put them until the following day or time when I can file them appropriately. You may find the Cozi Calendar's color-coded app, designed for and by moms, to be a great resource. Learn more at www.gygb.com.

• **Preview the next day:** Even though you have planned out, printed and reviewed the upcoming week, every night you still have to look at the next day. Schedules change and new events get added. Take a look before you go to bed and sleep peacefully, knowing what the day ahead holds.

• **Stay on task:** Work from your calendar. Knowledge is power. Being prepared ensures that you get where you need to go, on time and stress-free. As you preview the next day's calendar, pack any bags that need packing, gather up what's needed for the day and put everything by the door. This will prevent last minute chaos and keep you on schedule.

Are you beginning to get the picture? Your capture tool might be a clipboard system like mine, a smart phone, portable calendar in a binder, or something entirely different. Give it a try starting this week. It's important to start somewhere and you can modify your system with each passing day or week. Do what works best for you. Take a moment and jot down what your capture tool might look like.

THINK LIKE THIS GIRL

Control is power. Chaos and stress only live in an uncontrolled environment where it can bully and consume your life.

What ideas do you have for your own capture tool?

____

____

____

____

____

____

HOME EC TO GIRLNOMICS

Onto more exciting things: Let's talk cooking. Like it or not, someone has to feed the family. To eat healthy and keep your grocery bill down, it is important to pre-plan your week's meals. If at all possible, do not go to the grocery store without a plan. You will spend more money yet have nothing to eat. I spoke with a woman recently who said she spent $400-$500 a week on groceries for her family of four. In the same conversation she said her family eats out four to five nights a week because she finds it difficult to cook with her busy schedule. My immediate thought was, "Wow, I could save you at least $1500 a month!" That same week, David spoke with her husband, who had cancelled an upcoming vacation because the new kitchen the couple was putting in was going over budget. I couldn't help but mention how ironic it was they were putting in a new kitchen when the family ate out four to five nights a week and with a little planning they could save $1500 per month and use that for a vacation. Their lack of planning around food expense resulted in incredible waste. How much money could they be saving by planning ahead?

• **Plan your menu.** You're going to plan your meals the same way you update your capture tool. Spend 15 to 30 minutes each week coming up with a week's worth of menus and a grocery list. Look at your calendar to see who is home and what is happening, and put the main dishes you intend to cook on the actual calendar. Like many women, I get frustrated most weeks with what to cook. I have a few food magazines delivered each month (*Bon Appetit* is my favorite). I use cookbooks, and the old tried-and-true favorites I

How *This* Girl Does It:
Anonymous

Because of the way my parents raised me, I always believed I could do anything. I love hard. I fight hard. I play hard. But when I was four weeks postpartum with my second child, I felt I was in jeopardy of losing my girl. Then a good friend encouraged me to take a position as a divisional leader, going from managing 17 locations to 75. My husband encouraged me to go for the opportunity, and said that I didn't need to worry about things at home. He had us covered. "We're behind you 100%," he said, "but you need to figure this out." My friend told me, "You are fully capable of doing this! You can do it!" That gave me the confidence to apply for the position. It's ironic that the conversation I had with my friend, who is male, allowed me to gain my girl back. He gave me the leap of faith I needed by believing I could do that position and even move beyond it. Now I oversee 600 people.

Don't ever let anyone ever tell you that you can't have what you want. You can absolutely have what you want at any given time. Sometimes things won't be in equal proportion. But, absolutely, you can go for it!

grew up with. While it may at first seem like one more thing to do, a little planning time invested up front takes the stress out of feeding your family. Planning also allows you to build foods into your diet that are important to your family's health such as vegetables, fish, chicken, and fun desserts from time to time. Plan ahead and you won't be relying on unhealthy take-out and fast food.

When I married Dave I had no idea how to cook. I literally learned from a *Rachael Ray 30 Minute Meal* cookbook. Since then I've added in *Cooking Light* recipes (check out www.cookinglight.com) and had my mom teach me family favorites. I also grill a lot as I live in Florida when we have few wintery days. With the explosion of cooking shows, there is no reason you should have to spend more than 30 minutes in the kitchen preparing any meal. Be sure to seek out quick, healthy meal options. Each weekend I sit at the table, pull out magazines, cookbooks, recipes and my calendar. I plan breakfast and lunch options, and four to five dinners that allow for flexibility. I literally insert the dinner idea into each day as this seems to be the most challenging meal because it's at the end of the day and everyone is exhausted.

• **Make your list.** Going to the grocery store with a list keeps you on task and ensures you don't buy groceries that are not needed. It also helps you stay focused on your meal plan versus buying things you don't need. Note: Never go to the store on an empty stomach. You'll buy way more than you planned or need.

There are lots of great apps you can download on your smart phone or tablet that allow you to create and organize a grocery list according to the aisles in the stores. I personally use myShopi and can't shop without it. Check out this application as well as others, as they will save you a lot of time. Since they load on your phone, you will always have the list on hand should you stop unexpectedly at the store.

While it may not always be possible, try to go to the grocery when your kids are in school as you will spend less, be able to focus on the task at hand, and get your shopping done much faster. When planning your week, find a time to go when you are alone if at all possible. If your kids aren't in school yet and you have to take them, try to involve your child in finding items and turn it into a fun, educational experience.

• **Stay flexible.** Yes, you're going to work your plan. But plans don't always work out. As you implement this system you will see trends. Pay attention and modify as needed. If you're not using up fresh produce, for example, buy frozen vegetables instead. They won't go bad if you don't use them, and they have as much, if not more nutritional value than fresh.

• **Eat dinner as a family.** The most important advice I can give you as a mother is to eat dinner together at least three nights a week. As hard as this might be, do everything you can to make it happen. I realize with jobs, sports and school events this might seem virtually impossible but if there is a will, there is a way. You simply have to find it. Who says dinner can't be served at 8:30 at night a few times a week? If you can't do dinner, what about breakfast? Brainstorm, talk with your family and improvise to make it happen. We shut the television off, turn on music and light a candle most nights. You will notice I didn't say every night. We are working to get your girl back, not transform you into Wonder Woman! Setting the mood makes your meal more of an experience, and allows people to relax and slow down when eating. While your children might laugh at first, they will come to cherish this time.

• **Clean up**. Our household rule is that one person cooks, the other cleans up. Some nights Dave cooks and I clean up and some nights I cook and the kids clean up. In short, we share the workload. If you are a single mom, then you'll have to cook and clean up until your kids are old enough to help. My kids are seven and nine and they rotate the responsibility of clearing off the table and wiping it down while the other helps load the dishwasher. They like contributing and it's good for them, too. Make sure that the kitchen is clean before you go to bed. There is no better feeling as you go to bed, than to shut off the lights to a clean kitchen that smells good and is in order. This also helps ensure that you start the day off right come morning.

• **Establish a morning routine.** The best way to do this is to start the night before. Don't wait until the morning to pack lunches and prepare for the day. I used to run around wildly every morning, looking for shoes, papers, packing lunches, and finally realized that was just crazy. I remembered how my mother always had everything organized the night before. There were no surprises, no chaos, just a simple morning routine. Once I implemented this idea, the mornings went much smoother and I actually felt good going to bed knowing I was prepared for tomorrow. My motto is, control your day, don't let it control you.

Create a central location for the bags that are going with you in the car each morning. Have your keys laid out, shoes ready to go, clothes picked out and ironed if you choose to do so, and anything else that is part of your morning routine in order. While this will take some time to get used to, each time you prepare in advance, and wake up to a clean kitchen, organized bags, packed lunches, ironed clothes, and car keys at hand, you will feel like you can do anything. Start your day right. Also, instead of saying to the kids, "Hurry up, we're going to be late" say, "Let's get moving, we want to be on time." Always focus on what you want so your mind can help you to accomplish it. Positivity is power!

A PERSONAL SANCTUARY

As you work to get your girl back, it's important that your home be a place you long to return to, not one you dread entering. As a mother, you may find the workload of caring for a home overwhelming. I would like for you to consider what you can do to transform your home into your personal sanctuary, so you can feel some of the rewards of your hard labor. I suggest you start perhaps with a small space you can call your own. The peace you find there will eventually radiate to the rest of the house. What kind of home environment do you desire? How do you want to feel when you walk in the door? Let's take a few minutes to think about this.

How do you feel when you walk into the door of your home?

____

____

____

____

____

What would you *like* to feel when walking in the door of your home?

____

____

____

____

____

What are three things you can do so you get what you need when you walk in the door? Keep it simple. Here's an example: Every day without fail I would trip over shoes, backpacks and coats. Tired of yelling, I bought two beautiful, large reed baskets (one for each child) and placed them by the door. It took a couple weeks of prodding, but now my two kids are in the habit of dropping their stuff right into their basket. That one tiny change put me closer to having the sanctuary I wanted.

What small steps can you take today that will lead to greater calm tomorrow?

1. ____

____

2. ____

____

3. ____

____

Now let's think beyond day-to-day challenges and think about how you can create a home that reflects who you are. Many people never decorate their homes because the minute they move in they tell themselves it's temporary and that there is no sense in spending the time, money or effort on making something beautiful that they are quickly going to leave. I say, life is short. Don't wait! It's amazing what a coat of paint can do for a home and its inhabitants' spirits.

While considering what you can do to your entire house might seem overwhelming, think about the rooms you spend the most time in. For me, it's my bedroom, kitchen and office. My bedroom is painted in warm tones with pictures of Paris, France, my favorite city in the world, on the walls. I have scented candles I can light and a radio tuned to a station that plays soothing music. I keep my favorite books there, too. It's where I go to wind down after a long day. Not too long ago my daughter walked in while I was reading and said, "Wow, it's so peaceful in here, Mommy!" As she snuggled up to read her own book, I thought it profound that my nine-year-old understood the feeling the room created and sought it out. In my mind, I compare this to a master bedroom with laundry everywhere, a television blasting, white walls and toys scattered throughout. If this type of room makes you happy, by all means keep it that way. But if it doesn't, then you change it. Your girl needs it—and she's the one who'll help you make the changes. Remember that small changes can make big impacts. Start with one room and decide what you will do to begin the transformation process.

Room I'm going to start transforming:

____

____

I'm confident that you will so love the feeling your new environment creates that you will move from one room to the next, eliminating clutter, adding elements that bring comfort and slowly but surely making your home, room by room, a sanctuary your entire family will come to embrace.

MAID OR NO MAID?

If you have the money, the best gift you can give yourself is a housekeeper. I have helped many women make this tough decision. It's hard to justify spending $75 to $100 a week for something you could do yourself. Listen, Girlfriend: Take the money from your shopping or entertainment fund. I can easily live without that extra pair of shoes in exchange for Carmen, who has been my housekeeper for close to a decade. If this sounds wonderful to you, make it a goal and call around and get some quotes. This will quickly expedite the feeling of getting your girl back. Carmen's day—Thursday—is one of the best days of my week. She is like family and makes my life much better. While I pick up and declutter, she washes the sheets and does a thorough cleaning. When I first hired Carmen she came once a month. As my success grew I increased her to twice a month, and ultimately each week. Start small with the intention of growing big!

LAUNDRY

I've yet to meet a woman who has made peace with her laundry. Of all the things we do, this seems to be enemy number one. While I don't like to do it either, I have implemented a few simple systems that have made the process much easier. I start with doing a load of laundry every day. When someone first suggested this to me I yelled out loud, "There is no way I am going to do a load of laundry every day of my life. Are you crazy?" Yet here I am doing a load of laundry every day. Once I tried it, I realized laundry was much more manageable. Rather than doing ten loads on the weekend, I now strive to have all my laundry done by Friday. It's like a personal game.

My second tip: a laundry hamper with multiple bins. Teach your family to put their clothes in the bin by color and you've eliminated the chore of sorting. The third thing I do is fold and put the laundry away immediately. If I let it sit around it may somehow end up right back in the dirty laundry, even if it hasn't been worn. Fourth, I buy detergent that makes my clothes smell wonderful. I used to grab whatever was on sale. But then I noticed that the sheets and clothes at my mom's house always smelled amazing. When I asked what she used, she told me, and added, "It makes such a difference to doing laundry because I enjoy the scent so much!" Smart move: Rather than resent the chore, she found a way to enhance the experience. I found a detergent I love and now I love pulling the laundry out of the dryer while it's warm and being engulfed by the scent. As silly as it sounds, it's just one more thing to make a dreaded task more enjoyable.

The most important advantage to having a great laundry system is that you and your children will have enough clothes to wear. I believe some people shop compulsively because they look in their closets and come up empty because everything's dirty. Why go to the store to buy clothes you don't need when what you do need is in the hamper? You can do it, Girlfriend! Laundry is here to stay so get in the driver's seat and take control.

SCHEDULING

Women are run ragged. When your life gets to be all about running, your girl will run for the hills! If you'd told her she'd grow up to be an unappreciated cab driver, maid and cook, possibly while also working 40 to 50 hours a week outside the home, she'd have called you crazy. Yet here you are. While this is a very touchy subject, I plan to take it on. How in the world are you going to get your girl back if you're neck deep in an insane schedule?

You must make a decision. Do you want to get your girl back or not? If the answer is yes, then it's time to get honest about what you can and cannot do. Write down your daily routine or schedule for each day of the week. Be honest. What does a typical day look like for you?

Monday

____

____

____

____

Tuesday

Wednesday

Thursday

Friday

Saturday

Sunday

Go back and review your week. Did you include everything you do in a given day? Use the list below to prompt your memory:

- School drop off
- Errands
- Sporting practice or games
- Work
- Meal planning
- Grocery shopping
- Laundry
- Cleaning

- Cooking
- Date night
- Hobbies
- Volunteering
- Nursing
- Counseling
- Managing the family calendar
- Helping with homework

Okay. Now really look at all you do in a given week. How does that make you feel? Is this what you thought motherhood would be like? Is this what you want the next five, ten, or fifteen years to be?

Pretend that instead of 24 hours in a day, you have 25 and in order to get that extra hour, you must give it to yourself. What would you do with that extra hour if you had it every single day? Imagine that time has stopped, no one can see what you do or interfere, and it's just for you. What would you do with it?

____

____

____

____

____

____

Now imagine what this gift of time to yourself would feel like. What kind of impact would it make on your life?

____

____

____

____

____

TAKE CONTROL

Review your schedule again and think about what you can eliminate. This will be difficult, I understand, but anything worth having takes work. You are fighting for your girl's life. Get her back and everyone benefits, not just you. Does your daughter need to be involved in dance, cheerleading *and* gymnastics? Who is the boss here anyway? It's time to set limits. Kids are so overscheduled today they wouldn't know what to do if they had a day off. We are creating children who don't know how to be still, who are incapable of making choices, and who basically get anything they want. As a mother, you pay the price because in most cases, you have to drive, pay and wait and wait and wait while your children live their lives and you watch.

My rule is one sport at a time. Call me a horrible mom, but I refuse to let guilt rule my life. I love my children and will do anything for them but the reality is, scheduled activities can consume your life. One day I was at the YMCA while Noah's swim team was practicing. I went over to sit with the other mothers and decided to just listen. There were three different conversations going on among six women. Everyone was talking about her busy schedule, where she was going next, what she had to do for her child that week, and how difficult it was. In short, they were complaining and maybe even trying to one-up each other on motherly greatness. All I could think was, "If you don't like it, don't do it!" Don't complain about a situation you created and can control. Instead, eliminate something from your schedule. I know it's hard to hear. But your life is at stake here!

It's not heroic to sacrifice your life for your children. It's insane. Often people who do this are unhappy and unfulfilled. Some end up divorced because they have no time for their partners. If you choose to have this type of hectic lifestyle, then own it. Rather than complain, embrace it and enjoy every minute, knowing that you have made the decision to drive, pay and sit. If you want to stop the chaos, then make a decision right now and remove something from your weekly schedule and give yourself the gift of that one extra hour a day.

Are you with me? Just try this on for size: What one or two things can you remove from your weekly schedule? If you can muster up the strength to decide and follow through, you will be empowered and see your girl literally begin to reappear due to your strength to make the decisions needed to positively affect your life and your family's life. What can you eliminate or delegate?

I know what you're thinking. Your family may object. Let them. And be prepared to deal with their objections. Example: You tell your 12-year-old daughter she has to choose between soccer and ballet. "But moooom!" she says. "You let me do both last year!" You say, "This year is different. We need to slow our family down. You need to choose. Soccer or ballet."

____

____

____

____

I am so proud of you. This is not an easy topic. I am giving you permission to make some tough choices, the way my coaches and mentors did for me. Sometimes we need others to tell us what to do even when we already know. That's okay. It's important that you give yourself this gift. Do not pass this section up without taking some sort of action for the betterment of your life. That first step is hard, I know. But once you take it, you'll be so glad you did!

DISCIPLINE (YOURS!)

We've covered a lot of ground! The reality is that each segment of this chapter could be a chapter of its own. My goal is to show you how you can take big, all-consuming tasks and break them down into small, manageable pieces. Living a grand life might look easy but it takes a lot of work and, more importantly, the discipline to stick to the commitments you've made. How else will your girl be able to come forward and shine? If you decide to take action on meal planning, for example, stick to it. Build the necessary changes into your schedule and follow through daily and weekly until those tactics become habit. The reward will make the habit worthwhile. If you feel overwhelmed and don't know where to start, go back through your notes and look for the possible change that most speaks to you. Listen for your girl! She knows what you need!

What can you commit to right now?

What system will you put in place to ensure you follow through on this commitment?

What outcome do you expect?

Still struggling with fear that taking what you need might frustrate, anger or disappoint the ones you love? Think of the impact your decisions will have on your personal life. An overwhelmed spouse and mother typically complains a lot and is stressed out, burnt out and unhappy. Plain and simple, she's not enjoyable to be around. While others might not say it, I will. As you get your girl back, you will be positive, in control and energized. Your happiness will be infectious. Who would *you* rather be around? Someone who's frazzled? Or someone who's upbeat? You have the power to decide the type of life you will live. Your experience is a direct result of your choices and if you did not know this before, now you do.

EMBRACE LIKE THIS GIRL:
Chapter Summary

1. As women, we have been raised to believe that we have to do it all—ourselves. While this may have worked several decades ago, before women went into the work force, it doesn't work today. Learn to ask for help and accept it when others offer to give it.

2. The side effects of motherhood took what was left of your girl. With each increased responsibility and role you took on to be the world's best mom, your girl got buried deeper and deeper. You must fight to get her back. You will be a better, more complete person and in turn a more amazing mom than you ever imagined. And when you get your girl back, an amazing thing will happen—she'll love your kids, and your kids will love her. Oh, the fun you'll have!

3. Success is preparation meeting opportunity. Start your capture tool today.

4. While it seems easier to deal with breakfast, lunch and dinner when it's time to eat, last-minute planning actually creates a lot of unnecessary stress in your life. Plan ahead to improve your health, reduce stress and save money.

5. Get control of your home because your environment has a tremendous impact on your mindset and stress levels. A clean, organized home allows you to find what you need to run your life and will bring you great joy. Rather than try to escape your home, you will find yourself wanting to actually be there more often.

EMBRACE LIKE THIS GIRL:

Chapter Summary

(Continued)

6. Don't let laundry consume you. Do a load a day, fold it and put it away. You will feel more in control. And you'll stop buying unnecessary clothes to fill in the gaps when everything's dirty.

7. Your schedule is a direct result of choices you've made. If there's too much going on, make the decision to modify your schedule. While these decisions may be difficult, they must be made or you will ultimately pay the price.

8. Make time to live. While there is always something to do and somewhere to go, it's important to remember that life is not about the destination but the journey. Life is short. Don't let it pass you by.

chapter eight

WORK

LET'S TALK CAREER

I can still remember, as if it were yesterday, the day I stopped dreaming about my future and started making it happen. It was a definite moment in time when one door slammed closed and another opened. Sitting on the living room floor of my apartment, I felt a pull to my future, as if it were beckoning me to step in. I chose to listen. Surrounded by books, magazines, journals, markers, scissors, and unlimited possibility, I began to map out what I wanted my future to look like. I created my first dream book in hopes that my subconscious would show me its deepest desires and the path I was to follow. When an image spoke to me I put it into my dream book.

What I wanted more than anything was to be a motivational speaker. My heroes were Norman Vincent Peale, Anthony Robbins and Zig Ziglar. I have devoured every word they wrote. I started at the tender age of 14 when my mom first put Peale's *The Power of Positive Thinking* into my hands. I admired each author's ability to transform his thought process and, in turn, his actions and life. I understood early in life that the key to success lies in the ability to control my thoughts. Yet not until I started my dream book did I fully embrace my true power.

As I sat on my apartment floor flooded by visions of my future and the opportunities before me, I was certain of my destiny. I knew what I was born to do. I had just sold my corporate cleaning business and I was on a mission to step into my dream. That day I made a decision. I would never again take a job or start a business that did not in some way move me closer to my goal of being a motivational speaker.

As my first dream journal began to take shape, I was clueless to the power it would hold over my life and the magnitude of its strength. I knew I was meant for something more but didn't know exactly how to get there. The dream journal would serve as my guide. Below you can see that original goal I wrote:

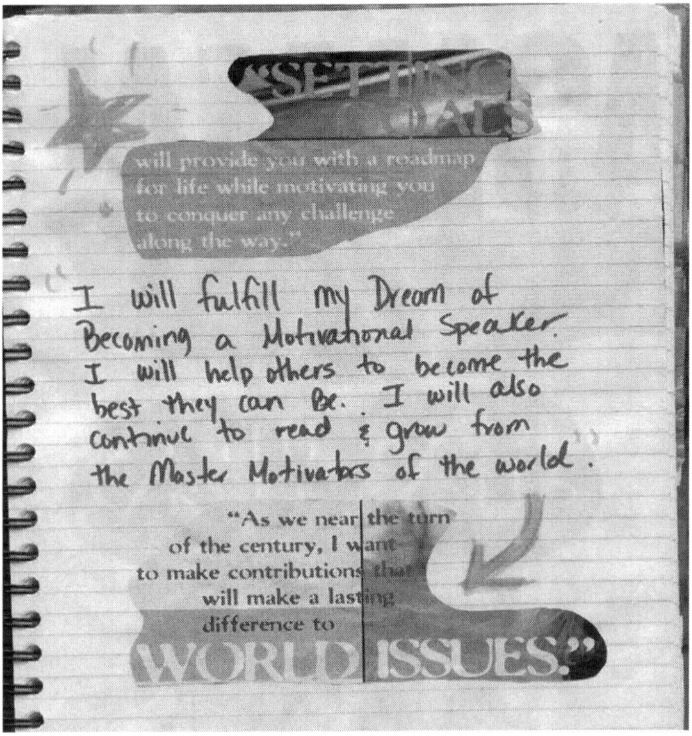

I was on fire. I had a desire and craving to teach, travel and embark on a lifelong learning adventure. I wanted it all, everything society told me I could never have because I was a woman, because I wasn't born into it, and because it simply was not expected of me. Instead, I decided to expect it of myself. I was going to be great. I, Traci Shafer, could be great.

HOW *THIS* GIRL DOES IT: MICHELE LEACH

I never really felt like I had my girl until now. The carefree, spontaneous side of me is emerging as I pursue my love of photography, where I can tell a story behind the pictures that I take. My parents always pushed me to "work, work, work." I never knew to have any goals outside of just getting a job. I don't think I was ever carefree or fun, or even dreamed about what I wanted to do until now. But now I know!

> THINK LIKE THIS GIRL
>
> *Expect greatness and you will get it.*

What about you? What is your deepest desire? What inspires, motivates or moves you in a way that nothing else does? What are you passionate about? You don't have to know how to translate these things into a career just yet. What you must do is put your finger on that one thing your soul craves more than anything else. What is it? Right now, jot down what comes to mind:

____

____

____

____

Stuck? Don't worry. You're an adult with a multitude of experiences behind you, and your mind may refuse to hand over the answer because it doesn't know how to use that one thing to make money and provide a living. Your mind is so caught up in the *how* that it's blocking you from seeing the *what.* It is critical that you let go, give up control, and just contemplate the questions I have asked. Once you have the answer, I assure you that the resources, tools, contacts, and ideas will naturally flow as you start to take ownership of your future. So don't worry about the how.

I created that first dream journal 20 years ago. I had one passion in mind and filled the journal with images that spoke to my soul. I chose pictures and writings that motivated and encouraged me to keep moving forward. Since that day, I have accomplished more than I ever thought possible. I am not only a motivational speaker but also a consultant who helps small, mid-sized and publically traded companies achieve massive growth in their businesses. I have spoken to audiences as small as ten and as large as 20,000. I have traveled all over the world and lived what seems a lifetime in my short 42 years here on earth. It's an amazing, dream-come-true life and I don't take a second of it for granted. Each day I am grateful that I took the time to map out my life and live by my own terms. It's time you do the same.

FIND YOUR WORK PURPOSE

The number one question I'm asked by clients is, "*How do I know what I am supposed to do with my life*?" People don't know what path to take. I always know that the answer to the individual's question lies deep within his or her subconscious. All I have to do is help the person fish it out.

If you have ever gone fishing, you know the patience it requires. You rise before the sun is up to get on the water while the fish are biting. Anxiously you bait the hook, cast the line and wait for a nibble.

The moment you feel a little tug on the line, you reel it in, only to discover that the hook is empty and the bait is gone. The fish that stole your bait was actually smarter than you! Hours can go by without a single catch. You cast and wait, cast and wait, and many times go home empty-handed. Yet on that one occasion you feel the tug and start to slowly reel in the line and realize you actually have caught something, it makes all the hours spent sitting and waiting worthwhile. As you pull the fish out of the water, especially if it's a big one, you're as excited as you would have been as a child. You yell with joy and insist that everyone admire your catch. That one fish makes your day!

You are about to go fishing for your dream. What are you supposed to do in your career? Let's fish for some answers.

Identify your natural talents and gifts.

The way to start creating your dream job is to look within. You will be most successful

How *This* Girl Does It: *Donna Cutting*

This is how my girl came back: Well into adulthood, I read *Speak and Grow Rich* by Dotty Walters. I began a new career speaking on employee engagement, and someone asked me what I would charge. This was the first time I realized I could make money for speaking! Since 1999, my consulting firm has grown around the idea of Red Carpet customer service. I started tapping into my love of the entertainment field, and my performance side came out. I ended up writing *The Celebrity Experience,* based on the idea of "star treatment" and how that related to customer service. The research was fascinating and I was so excited about it!

What I do best is get up on stage and get everyone excited. I love it! I love our Red Carpet kickoffs. That's me and my girl putting on the talent show of my life! I love what I do. I love my clients. I am thrilled when I see my clients change, and embrace the changes in their companies from what they have learned. I feel like I'm eight years old, kicking my heels, and dreaming my way through life!

when you use your God-given talents. Every person has a gift to offer the world. What better way to use it than in your work? You have to work every day anyway, so why not do something you love and get paid top dollar to do?

I want you to start investigating your natural talents. Think back to compliments you've received and conversations you've had with others about how you excel or do well. Perhaps you're an excellent cook who brings incredible design flair to the table. Maybe your gardens stop people in their tracks and enter an alternate reality of peace and tranquility. Or perhaps you're an ace at convincing customer service departments to pay attention to your concerns. Don't dismiss these things as career opportunities just because they're easy for you. This is what I'm talking about. Work should not be hard or forced. You want to focus on what comes naturally to you and is easy but to others perhaps not so simple. Consider what brings you the most joy and that is something you would do every day if you could.

When I was in grade school, every report card sent home said: "Traci talks too much." While I was embarrassed and ashamed by this scolding, it was true. I loved to talk. As an adult, I embraced that gift and now I generate millions of dollars a year because of it! Thank goodness I didn't listen to people who could have stifled this gift.

Put the logical side of your brain aside for the moment. In this space and time you are simply going to put pen to paper. What are your gifts or natural talents?

____

____

____

____

____

____

I realize this is a difficult exercise. I remember doing this myself. It was hard! Here's some help. Circle the ideas below that speak to you in any way:

Gardening Cooking Singing Acting Fitness
Accounting Photography Computers Fundraising
Talking Comedy Counseling Writing Minister
Animals Sports Decorating Sewing Teaching
Technology Reading Traveling

Did you identify any triggers that stimulated your thought process? At the end of this chapter, make it a point to browse through magazines or go the bookstore and flip through books that speak to you. Purchase a few and begin to go through them, cutting out images for your own dream book. Don't worry about why you like certain pictures or what they mean, just cut and paste them into a journal or onto a poster board. You can also go to Google Images and search words that you would like to see images of such as peace, gardening, exercise and so on. Hundreds of beautiful images will pull up. I do this for myself and my children. I print those images that inspire me or that I feel will speak to my kids, laminate them, and tape them to our mirrors in the bathroom. You can do the same thing with inspirational quotes or favorite sayings in an effort to retrain your brain. Each time you read the posting your mind will transform a bit more.

While you seek answers, accept the ideas that come to you and embrace them. Rule nothing out. Allow yourself to be open and receptive to what comes forth. This is so important as your mind will direct you toward your destiny. Do not stand in its way. Realize that while you may want an answer today, you may not get it for a week, a month or a year. The more open you are to answers, the

How *This* Girl Does It:
Kathy Brentlinger

I worked in nursing homes for a long time, and I didn't like what I saw. There were too many tasks taking nurses away from patients' bedsides and chained to a desk. I found that I wasn't very happy under those conditions, and began to think about starting my own company. I loved the idea of people being able to live in a nice apartment, surrounded by their own things—not sharing half of a room with a stranger—and being able to have nursing care brought to them.

Seventeen years ago, when I started Senior Care Management, I saw myself standing on a cliff, ready to leap. God's hand was coming down, and I pictured myself grabbing His hand. For years, I kept diaries of what I saw that worked well in the companies I worked for, and things that I thought they didn't do very well. I was able to start my company with the savings that I had, a little bit from my parents, and by doing lots of nursing shifts. I prayed about my company a lot. I didn't start it without really feeling like it was the right thing to do, or knowing that it was going to be hard work. I knew that I would rather work for myself than companies who had policies and procedures I didn't believe in.

sooner they will come. It's going to take time to give up control and allow life to work on your behalf. While you may not understand this now, you will later.

How do you feel? Are you emotional, drained, excited or frustrated? Welcome any emotions you have because they are proof you are alive and on the path to finding your true work purpose.

HOW TO TURN TALENTS AND GIFTS INTO A CAREER AND INCOME

As you start to identify your direction, a little voice is probably going to pipe up and say:

- » Who will hire me to do this?
- » Aren't there people with more experience?
- » Can I actually get paid to do this?
- » Where do I start?
- » Am I crazy?

Yes, self-doubt is going to creep into your mind like a snake quietly slithering through the grass. You must learn to control it. The moment you tell yourself that you can never turn your passion into a dream, turn that thought around. Restate it into a fact about what you can do. Not, "It's too much work to become a spiritual counselor." Instead, "I am fully capable of doing the work to become a spiritual counselor." Continue to mold your mind toward the thoughts you want it to have, not those that come naturally. Remember, you are in control. This is your mind, your life, your dream, your future. Fight for it!

GET A JOB OR WORK FOR YOURSELF?

As I help you move toward your dream career, I want you to be aware of your options. While you may think the only option is to work for a company or a boss, that's not true. If you live in America, you know you're in the greatest country on earth and in this country anything is truly possible. If you live in another country, then you have to have the courage to be the change you seek. You must forge a path not only for yourself but for your children. If it is absolutely impossible or illegal to have your own business as a woman in your country then I will at least help you find a middle ground where you can utilize your passion to bring joy to your daily job.

I am in America and I can only draw from my own experiences.

Yet I have a tremendous passion for women all over the world and have always felt a connection to the struggles of women who do not have the same opportunities as I do. I don't squander my opportunities because I understand how fortunate I am to have been born here, in the great USA. In a way, I do more because many women are repressed in their part of the world. It's my way of honoring them, by seizing the opportunity I have. If you are in another part of the world and don't have equal rights, please know that I am here in your corner, fighting for you. If you do live in the USA or in a country where you have equal rights, stop for a moment and really process what this means. Use this as fuel to honor those women who are less fortunate, and make your dreams a reality.

What are your options? You can work for someone else, be it a small business or large corporation, or you can work for yourself. Don't worry about which is right for you at this time, just ponder the possibility and know that it is there.

This is the age of the entrepreneur! There is no better time in our history than right now to start a business. You can do just about anything with a computer and a telephone. The good news is that if you can't afford a computer you can still go to a library and use one

How *This* Girl Does It: *Anonymous*

For me, it's not, "fake it till you make it." It's "fake it till you *become* it." I'm learning the power of posing and posturing. Every day I look in the mirror, not to admire myself, but to really look at how other people perceive me. What should my body language look like? This gets me in the right mind frame. Even if I don't wake up feeling positive and confident, I look in the mirror and do some power poses.

I also have a dream board, to keep my eye on the prize. Perspective for me includes being a comprehensive woman, using a 4 M formula:

M: Go in the boardroom and be like Meg Whitman. Speak articulately and people will look at you like you are an expert in for free. If you don't have a telephone, odds are you can access one from a friend or family member. You will notice that I didn't say you need money. I have started five businesses from scratch, and only one of them utilized funds that I generated from the sale of another business. What you do need is passion, drive, a strong work ethic, follow-through, and the belief that you will succeed.

Let's look at your choices. If you get a job, you will have a boss and will work set hours and perform agreed upon tasks in exchange for your services. You will have certainty so long as you have the job. You'll have a steady paycheck, and probably health insurance or a benefit plan. You will wake up every day and build someone else's business.

On the other hand, if you start a business, you will be the boss, work long hours, perform a broad variety of tasks that you love, as well as some you despise. In all likelihood, for a period of time you won't be paid for your time, energy, and effort. You will live a life of uncertainty, have unstable finances, and at times, no benefits. You will wake up every day and build your business and in due time, you will reap the rewards that far exceed building another person's business. There is one catch—the business you start, in order to succeed,

your field. People will respect what you have to say because you have earned it.

M: Be Mary Poppins in the nursery, someone who creates great memories for her kids, creating environments where they feel secure and loved and well-adjusted.

M: Be Madonna in the bedroom. Don't be the frumpy mom who says "I'm tired," or gains 45 pounds and stays that way because you've had a kid. It's not going to kill you to put on a lacy bra and a garter belt and get into bed with your husband. Get rid of those elastic jeans and the ponytail.

M: Be Martha Stewart in the kitchen. Create great food and entertain your friends so they know that they're important to you.

must be centered on your natural gifts and talents. You may need to hire or contract out those tasks you don't know how to do (such as accounting) but in the end, if you stay true to your purpose, you will succeed.

> THINK LIKE THIS GIRL
>
> *If you are not failing, you are not trying hard enough.*

JOB OR BUSINESS?

Based on your work in this chapter, what most speaks to you right now? Would you prefer to get a job or own a business? Don't worry about which answer is the correct one. You are working on your life, brainstorming, pondering, and starting to figure things out. Right now you are starting the conversation.

HOW TO TRANSLATE TALENT INTO INCOME

If you decide to start a business, odds are you'll have to moonlight—hold a steady-paying job while you build your business on the side. I waited tables at night when I started my first training company and worked on my business during the day. It was hard, but I can tell you without a doubt that the sacrifice was worth it. Depending on your passion, you will know when you'll need to work on your business and therefore when to schedule a paying job. Striking that balance will dictate the kind of job you take.

Let's say you're a chef at a local restaurant. You work the day shift and make $48,000 per year. While you like your job and got into it because you love cooking, you're burnt out. From a demanding boss to customers who are impossible to please, you feel unappreciated, underpaid and downright exhausted at the end of each work day. After work you go home to cook again but this time for your family who are also demanding and oftentimes unappreciative of the meal prepared. You like the ideas presented in *Get Your Girl Back* but are not sure how to move into a position that brings joy and income.

If you prefer to continue working for someone else, you might consider moving from a chef in a busy restaurant to a school where you can teach upcoming chefs the trade. In this environment you would work at a slower pace, have room for creativity, garner appreciation and an income. If you prefer your own business, you might start a catering business on the side. Start very informally by telling your friends and family that you are available for catering or personal chef services. Odds are these people will support you and hire you because they know of your talent in the kitchen. What will start as one job, probably at a fraction of what you deserve, will manifest into many jobs at a rate you never imagined people would pay for catering services. These are two examples of how you can translate a passion into a more satisfying job or even a business. As you express your natural gifts and talents, word will spread, opportunity will present itself and you will quickly begin to move toward a career you never imagined possible. Will this happen overnight? Probably not, but it will happen. Like fishing, this new path will require patience.

THE REWARD

The average person in the United States works at minimum, 40 hours a week. This is a huge chunk of time. I don't need to quote studies and statistics to tell you that if you're unhappy in your job you'll be unhappy at home. Like it or not, most people take work home with them. If the overflow is not physical, it's mental. The overall state of your happiness depends on you creating a career that is worthwhile and taps into your God-given abilities. No matter how successful you are today, you will be much more successful tomorrow if you incorporate your natural talents and gifts into your career. You will have greater job satisfaction, make more money, experience more joy, improve your relationships and start each day with a sense of purpose.

While you might be afraid to take a risk and move toward a new career path, contemplate the potential reward waiting for you. When that risk pays off, the reward will be tremendous and even more meaningful because of the courage it took to do it. When I started my first business, a corporate janitorial service, it required a huge risk. I was on the fast track in retail management. I loved what I was doing but felt the calling to give it up to help my mom grow her struggling cleaning company. That decision ultimately led me to the company I have today. I have balance and flexibility in my life. I work from home, schedule my own hours and spend as much time as I want with my children and Dave. My risk-taking paid off and yours will too.

What if you fail? Whenever I contemplate a tough decision, I look at the best case scenario and the worst case scenario. If I can't live with the worst case scenario then I don't take the risk. If it will be uncomfortable or difficult but I can live with the worst case scenario, then I go for it. Only you will be able to decide what's right for you. The thought of failure can be paralyzing. But don't let fear rob you of your dream. I have failed many times. Each time I got back up and fought for my dream. Failure is just life delivering a hard lesson. If you learn from the lesson, you will move on. If you don't learn, the lesson will be repeated, and that is not fun. I've always been a fast learner. Every person who has succeeded has a string of failures behind her. It's part of the journey.

YOUR GIFT AND ITS IMPACT ON THE WORLD

While you might be humble and downplay your natural talents and gifts, you have the ability to impact people's lives in a big way. Think of the kindergarten teacher who had a high paying job as a pharmaceutical rep yet who had a way with children and loved education. Perhaps you or your child benefited from her courage to turn in her high paying, high respect job for the unappreciated, underpaid, demanding job of teaching. This person has the ability to impact a child's entire life.

If it were not for the gift of my personal coach, Sue Youngs, I would have never written this book. It was her gift of listening, counseling and advising that forever changed my life. If not for her, I would have had Paris and continued working 60-hour weeks. I would have missed out on Paris's first word, first step—maybe even her first day of school. Because of Sue's gift and its impact on my life I've not missed a moment. I am a better person, mother, entrepreneur, daughter, friend and wife because of Sue. Her gift changed my life.

Imagine, a year from now, depending on your gifts, that someone could be saying that about you. Whether it's the cake you baked for someone's wedding or the website you built for someone's company, your talent will have a direct impact on another life. How will that feel? Are you getting excited?

THINK LIKE THIS GIRL

God has more planned for you than you can ever imagine for yourself.

WORK LIKE THIS GIRL:

Chapter Summary

1. While it might be challenging to tap into your gifts and identify how to parlay those into a job or business, it is imperative you take the time needed to work through this process. Everyone has a natural talent or gift. Your goal is to translate that into a career for a life of purpose and fulfillment.

2. Don't worry so much about how you are going to turn your gifts into gold. Instead, focus on how best to use your gifts or talents to start the beginning of something great. Know that when you are true to yourself and use the talent God gave you, you will be successful beyond your wildest dreams. Take a leap of faith and walk toward your dream until you're ready to run.

3. Moving from where you are today to where you want to be tomorrow will not be easy. Anyone who has ever achieved anything great has worked for it. You will have to do the same. You may have to work two jobs, sacrifice material items you normally enjoy, or do work that you might consider beneath you. There is a price to pay for the reward you will reap. You must place the price and the reward on the scale and determine which is more valuable.

4. Your gift has the ability to change not only your life but also the lives of others. Never underestimate your ability to make a difference. You are worthy, you are deserving, and you do have something of incredible value to give to the world. In return you will be blessed beyond measure.

chapter nine

MANAGE

LET'S TALK FINANCES

You can't *do* better until you *know* better. This is never more true than when it comes to finances. As you strive to get your girl back, it is vital that you get control of your money. I've been on every end of the spectrum when it comes to finances and will tell you point blank that you don't need money to be happy, but it sure does make you much more comfortable.

People like to downplay the power of money, yet every aspect of life revolves around having it or not. The quality of food you eat depends on how much money you have. If you have money you can afford to buy produce that is free of poisonous pesticides. If you don't, you are going to purchase whatever is cheapest and odds are that produce will have up to 30 different pesticides. If given a choice, which produce would you rather eat? The school your child attends more than likely is a direct reflection of your financial situation. People who live in upper or middle class neighborhoods have an absolute advantage when it comes to education over people who live in the inner city or poverty-stricken neighborhoods. If given a choice, would you rather send your child to an A-rated school that is well maintained, has high parent involvement and acceptable class size, or a school that is dilapidated, overcrowded, gang-ridden and F-rated? Let's be honest. Money matters. If I can help you understand how to make and keep more and in turn improve your quality of life, then the purpose of this chapter will have been served.

MONEY DEFINED

Money is severely misunderstood. By dictionary definition it is "*any article or substance used as a medium of exchange, measure of wealth or means of payment.*"[1] By human definition it is *happiness*. The goal of this chapter is to help you fully understand what money is and how to use it properly to fuel your life.

How many times have you heard someone say, "*If I just had more money everything would be better*"? There is a misconception that money solves all problems. In reality money can actually make problems worse. Consider the lottery. Over two million people play each week, yet the odds of being the jackpot winner are approximately 1 in 14 million (13,983,816 to be exact). Of those who do win, 70% will squander their winnings in a few years. In the process, they will see family and friendships destroyed and the financial security they hoped for disappear. You decide. Does money make people happy? Would winning the lottery make you happy?

I live by the motto, "*I am my own lottery ticket.*" I don't play the lottery and have no desire to win it. I believe that there is something to be said for good old-fashioned hard work, for earning money, and feeling the sense of pride that comes with creating wealth. While I am certain that people who won the lottery thought they would handle the money differently and that their lives would not fall apart, in most cases they did. For me, the gain of winning the lottery is simply not worth the pain and loss. I love my family and friends too much to exchange them for a few million or even a hundred million dollars. What about you?

1 Dictionary.com, s.v. "money," accessed June 4, 2015, http://dictionary.reference.com/browse/money.

How *This* Girl Does It: *Julie Podewitz*

I grew up very simply. We lived in tract housing in Detroit. My dad was a teacher, my mom was a stay-at-home mom. We had one car. When I went to college, I remember thinking, "Oh my gosh. I'm poor."

I was always extremely motivated to make money. In college, I worked three jobs to get by. I hated feeling so stressed about money. And that's why I love sales. I'm motivated by revenue. When you focus on what you love to do, the money will follow. I still struggle with, "What if this all goes away?" but I use that to motivate me. To gain confidence and financial freedom, I've learned:

- Don't spend more than you make.
- Forgive yourself. It was hard for me to admit that I like to make money. But I've resolved not to sabotage myself. I recently treated myself to a nice piece of luggage, and I told myself not to feel guilty about it. Give yourself permission to love and to be loved, to be treated well.
- Dare to succeed. I think women struggle to allow themselves to be assertive without being called a "bitch." It's okay to be feminine. It's okay to make as much, or more, than men do. One of my GYBG moments was treating my mom to a trip to England, and later to the Mediterranean with my daughter.
- Take care of yourself. I love to treat myself to the spa once a month. Date nights with my husband, time with my daughter, exercise, reading and alone time are ways that I take care of my girl.

It's part of the American dream to win the lottery. As you strive to get your girl back, I want to make sure that this pipe dream—winning the lottery—is not still lurking in your mind. Once you erase any probability of winning the lottery, you will realize that you too are your own lottery ticket, and that if your financial situation is going to change, it's you who's going to change it. Take a moment and answer these questions:

THINK LIKE THIS GIRL

When it comes to money, live by this motto: I am my own lottery ticket!

If someone were standing in front of you with a suitcase containing ten million dollars and you had to pick either the suitcase or your significant other, which would you pick? ____________________

If that same person took you on a journey and showed you the most beautiful home you could ever imagine, the very one you always dreamed of, took you for a spin in the most amazing car you ever sat in, offered to give you a wardrobe of new clothes, to include any designer brands you wanted, and a black American Express card with no limit, all yours in exchange for the relationship you have with your family, would you accept it? ____________________

If you answered yes, then you probably should play the lottery. If you answered no, then it's time to stop playing the lottery once and for all. By playing the lottery, I don't just mean the state lottery but also the dream of winning a lawsuit, hitting it big in Vegas, or marrying someone who can solve all your problems with his bank account. Make a decision that you will not play again and that instead you will map out a plan for your life that will provide the money you need to be fulfilled and happy. Every woman is different. Some want money for a sense of financial security and peace of mind in knowing their children will go to college, the bills will be paid, and there will be funds for retirement. Some women could care less about those things and instead desire money for a fabulous wardrobe, a nice car, jewelry and exotic vacations. You might prefer something else. Only you can know. But whatever it is, you must make peace with money and understand its purpose in your life.

Take a moment and define what money means to you.

a. How much money do you currently make or bring into your household?____________________________

b. How much money do you ideally want to make or have as an annual household income? ______________

c. What is the gap? (a-b=c)?

____

How *This* Girl Does It: *Kathy Brentlinger*

After my divorce, I decided to accept that I was not going to be a wealthy woman. I had to make good, smart decisions for my four children and myself. I needed to look at myself as my own CEO and banker. Were the things I was spending money on really necessary? Were they really going to improve our lives? Were they going to teach my kids how to be good people—or just how to be consumers? From a young age, I never got into credit card debt. I had one credit card and that was just for emergencies. For me, it was a more positive experience to save and pay cash for something than to use credit and end up resentful about the bill and the interest charges.

I would advise women to live within your means, save for things, and figure out what you like to do. Get a job in the area that you enjoy. Make financial decisions that are going to enhance your well-being and not cause a lot of stress. As head of my own company, I supervise 60-75 employees and oversee 150 patients, and I absolutely love what I do.

> THINK LIKE THIS GIRL
>
> *Money can't make you happy. But it can make you more comfortable.*
> *Better yet, it can fuel your girl's vision.*

If you were to close the gap and meet your income goal, what specifically would you do with the additional money (be specific)?

____

____

____

____

____

____

____

____

What kind of impact would this have on your life (again, be specific)?

____

____

____

____

Would you say that this money would make you happier or more comfortable (pick one)? ____________

Would the benefit of having this additional money be worth the pain or effort it takes to close the income gap and get there? ____________

Is your goal realistic? ______________________

If the goal is not realistic, meaning it is a pipe dream, think about what might be realistic for you but also a stretch. What income gap would you like to close in the next one to two years and what impact will that have on your life?

What does money mean for you and your life?

THINK LIKE THIS GIRL

If you want to feel rich, just count the things that money can't buy.

GRATITUDE

While most everyone could benefit from more money, I would like to look at what you have right now. It might not be what you desire—to attract more—but you must first be grateful for what you currently have. Rather than put focus on what you don't have, can't buy, or how money is ruining your life, start giving thanks for what you have and thinking thoughts of abundance. To attract money you must have a healthy relationship with it.

In previous chapters I shared the importance of a positive thought process and how smart the brain really is. If your thought is, "I don't have enough money," your mind immediately thinks, "Don't have money, don't have money, don't have money" and manifests in your life as your not having money. When you begin to express gratitude and think abundant thoughts, such as, "I am grateful for the abundance in my life," your mind thinks, "Abundance, abundance, abundance," and in turn you manifest abundance in your life.

In every stage of my life, no matter how difficult it was financially, I gave thanks. I found the good and put focus on it. When my prized green Ford Mustang was repossessed, I was late on my rent, and had nothing more than soup in the cabinet to eat, I was giving thanks for the business I was starting, for the mind that allowed me to dream, and for the man by my side. I never gave in to the temptation to lament or dwell on the fact that my car was gone or that my rent was late. When my car was repossessed I did cry when I woke up and found it missing, but I set to work immediately figuring out how I was going to get another car. The used Honda Civic I purchased was nowhere near as fun to drive but it got me where I needed to go and I kept moving forward. I continued to focus on the future, where I was going, what I hoped to accomplish, the blessings I had in my life, and those yet to come. I challenge you to do the same, no matter how difficult your circumstances.

MANAGE THE FUNDS YOU HAVE

What is your annual household income right now? ___________

Below, I provided a chart to determine where your money goes each month. The first step to financial freedom is understanding what money you have and where it is going. There is a law I have witnessed throughout my life: If you can't manage the money you have, whether it is $30,000 or $100,000, you will not be able to manage more. How many times have we all seen someone get a raise, only to spend every additional dime and still be broke?

> THINK LIKE THIS GIRL
>
> *If you can't learn to manage the money you have, you will never be able to manage more.*

Income

Wages and Salaries

Wage Earner 1____

Wage Earner 2____

= Total Wages and Salaries__________________________

+ Interest and Dividends _______________
+ Royalties, Commissions and Rents ___________
+ Other Income _______________

= A. Total Income ______________________________

Taxes (can use a percentage of income such as 30-35% depending on your tax bracket)

Federal Income and Social Security ______________
State ______________

= B. Total Income Taxes _________________________

C. Take-Home Pay (line A minus line B) ______________

Expenditures

Living Expenses

Housing

+ Rent ____________

+ Mortgage Payments ______________

+ Utilities _________________

+ Maintenance ______________

+ Real Estate and Property Taxes _________________

+ Fixed Assets—furniture, appliances, etc.

____

+ Other Living Expenses __________________

= D. Total Housing Expenditures ___________________

Food

+ Food and Supplies _______________

+ Restaurant Expenses _____________

= E. Total Food Expenditures ______________________

Clothing and Personal Care

+ New Clothes ________________
+ Cleaning _________________
+ Tailoring _______________
+ Personal Care, Hair Care ________________
+ Other Clothing and Personal Care __________________

= F. Total Clothing and Personal Care _____________________

Transportation

+ Automobile Purchase _______________
+ Payments _______________
+ Gas, Tolls, Parking ________________
+ Automobile Registration/Tags/Stickers ______________
+ Repairs ________________
+ Other Transportation Expenses ___________________

= G. Total Transportation Expenditures _______________

Recreation

+ Movies, Theatre, Sporting Events __________________
+ Club Memberships ___________________
+ Vacations ____________________
+ Hobbies ____________________
+ Sporting Goods ___________________
+ Gifts _____________________
+ Reading Materials ________________
+ Other Recreation Expenses __________________

= H. Total Recreation Expenditures __________________

Medical Expenditures

+ Doctor ________________
+ Dental ________________
+ Prescription Drugs and Medicines ________________

= I. Total Medical Expenditures ____________________

Insurance Expenditures

+ Health ________________
+ Life ________________
+ Automobile ________________
+ Disability ________________
+ Liability ________________
+ Other Insurance Expenses ________________

= J. Total Insurance Expenditures ________________

Other Expenditures

+ Educational Expenditures ____________________
+ Child Care ____________________
+ Other Expenses ____________________

= K. Total Other Expenditures ____________________

L. Total Expenditures (add lines D-K) ________________

M. Income Available for Savings
(subtract line L from line C) ____________________

As you can see, there are lots of things to spend money on. In fact, the more money you make, the higher these category expenses go.

TIME TO CUT, GIRL!

Grab a red pen or a color that is different from the one you used to complete the financial exercise. The next step is not going to be easy, but it's going to help you gain more power every day. You are in control, you have the ability to make tough choices and live by them. Go back through your budget and modify any expenses that allow for wiggle room. For example, while you may not want to, could you spend $800 a month on groceries rather than $1000 by planning your menu and grocery list as you learned in Chapter 7? Could you use coupons? Could you cut entertainment by $300 a month by making lattes at home and renting movies and making popcorn rather than going to the theater and dropping $60? While you may not want to and it may not be easy, is it possible?

Go through your list again with your red pen and modify or adjust each category where possible.

> THINK LIKE THIS GIRL
>
> *Think, "I don't have enough," and you won't. Think, "I am so blessed," and you will be.*

In revising your list, take a moment to add up the savings you identified. In total, with sacrifice and modifications, how much could you save if you really put your back into it? ______________________

Go through your list one more time. Can anything else be changed? This is a means to an end. To get more tomorrow you have to do more today. You are moving in the right direction.

How much in total savings did you come up with? ______________

In reviewing your finances, do you have more or less money than you thought? __________

How does that make you feel?______________________________

____

Look back at your income goal. Take that number and put it in the space provided and then deduct the added savings you just identified in your cost cutting exercise. Did you move any closer?

a. Income goal:____________________________

b. Identified savings:________________________

c. Total amount needed to hit income goal_________

Whatever this number, own it. Do not be intimidated. Do not be afraid. You will achieve this goal. You have the knowledge acquired throughout the pages of this book to get your girl back and take ownership of your life. In this chapter you are taking the tough steps required to break through financial imprisonment that has had women in a chokehold for generations.

GOODBYE GUILT, HELLO ABUNDANCE

It's important to address the impact that guilt has on women and money. Guilt about making and spending money, a taboo subject for most people, has kept many women from reaching their true financial potential.

I have spoken to hundreds of thousands of women all over the US and Canada. And I discovered that the most common things holding them back from financial success is their fear and guilt. It's as if women have created their own glass ceiling, built from years of being told that financial success is wrong. There is a stigma about how much a woman should make—and it better not be more than her husband! It's as if women have their place in the world and it is not as financial head of the household. It takes a very strong and confident man to be married to a woman who makes more than he does. Women know this and have been brainwashed to believe they should hold back on their earning power. If a woman does become a higher earner, this myth goes, there will be hell to pay: A failed marriage, the death of a child, loss of a parent, and every other imaginable disaster you can think of. Just writing these words brings me chills—these concepts are *so* inbred in our culture!—and I have to use total mind control to force them out of my brain.

If something devastating is going to happen, it's going to occur anyway, not as a result of your financial success. The idea that doing well will cause tragedy is a load of crap and you must get that idea out of your mind. Just as a man has the right to make unlimited money, so does a woman—and that means you. Whether you want to make $60,000 a year or $600,000 a year, it's up to you. The more money you make, the greater impact you can have on the world around you. It's important to begin seeing money as a tool that can bring good to the world at large rather than bad to yours.

Drop the superstitious stuff and focus instead on the good that money can bring. How might you change the world around you when you hit or exceed your income goal? Whether you help a local food bank, your church, or a teacher in desperate need of school supplies, how might your ability to make more money impact not just you but others around you? Take a moment and jot down your ideas.

How would those you give to feel? What kind of impact might you have on their lives?

Which is better? To let guilt and fear limit your financial potential? Or to focus on the good you can do upon hitting your financial goals? It may take some time to really believe this, and the only way to transform your thoughts (and in turn your actions) is to put the focus on what you want. Write down a positive affirmation that speaks to you and that will help you to permanently eliminate the guilt over being a woman making money. Examples: *I do beautiful work for beautiful money. I deserve to earn what I am worth. I am willing to receive infinite abundance. My work is precious and so am I.*

Now write your financial affirmation:

____

____

____

____

____

____

I challenge you to write this affirmation on a notecard or piece of paper, right now, and post it where you can see and read it daily. You have to retrain your brain and with every reading you will move closer to believing this affirmation.

FINANCIAL SYSTEMS

There are tools I have created over the years that have empowered me to better manage money, whether I had a little or a lot. These systems will help you to gain control over your finances as well. Take a look, then implement the systems that make the most sense. Your goal is to operate in baby steps.

Create three bank accounts. If possible, have your paycheck (as well as any other funds you receive such as child support, dividends or rental property income) deposited automatically. Most companies will deposit paychecks in up to two different bank accounts and for a modest fee, more. We are putting everything possible on autopilot because the concept, "out of sight, out of mind" creates structure and reduces chaos.

1. Expense Account. Typically the largest, this will be used for fixed monthly expenses—things you must pay no matter what, such as rent or mortgage, utilities, insurance and car.

2. Spending Account. This represents your discretionary spending. You should allot a number—it could be $100, it could be $1000—to things such as eating out, clothing and entertainment. This account has more flexibility, meaning if you have it to spend, you do and if you don't, you don't. Whatever the amount is, you spend it and no more. You must learn to live within the parameters of this account without dipping into the others.

3. Savings Account. If you do not have a savings account, open one, no matter how small. It is important to start somewhere. If this is literally impossible, then set a goal to open one by a specific date. It's not the amount that matters, it's the discipline of putting money away and watching it accumulate. Ten dollars a month is not too little. As you begin this habit, you will naturally desire to put more and more away because you will see that this is the one pot of money that no one has his hand in, it's yours.

Here's what a month might look like:

Net Pay:	$3,000
Expense Account:	$2,500
Spending Account:	$400
Savings Account:	$100

Pay bills online. Most banks offer this service for free. Paying your bills online ensures that they are paid on time and late fees are avoided. Online banking will help you be more disciplined in managing your money.

Stop using credit cards. If you don't have the money to buy something, don't buy it. Credit cards have had a devastating impact on women's lives. Once you're in debt it's nearly impossible to get out, because the interest rates are criminal and banks are invested in keeping you hooked. Keep one card for travel and real emergencies only. Order a debit card for your spending account and use this card exclusively for your purchases. Once your spending account is low, you know you're at your limit and have to slow down to keep on track with your budget.

I wouldn't order a debit card for your expense account. Not having easy access will reduce the temptation to withdraw money that's already earmarked for something else. It's important to set yourself up to succeed and these details, though small, are designed to support you, reduce temptation, and ensure you hit your financial goals. If you have four or five credit cards in your purse right now, get them out and cut up all but one. What is the purpose of multiple cards anyway? The more you have, the more likely you are to use them and max them out. One card, one limit, one payment is your immediate goal.

Ultimately, you're shooting for no credit card debt at all. Each time you use a credit card, I challenge you to think about the cost of that particular purchase. What are you going to pay in stress, fear, lost sleep and pure panic when the bill is due and funds are short? If you were paying with cash instead of credit, would you still make the purchase? Even when I'm shopping and see lots of things I want, I simply don't yield to impulse. Unless I've planned ahead to buy something specific, I look only, then just walk away. If an item weighs on my mind for a few days, then I know it's something I really want and I may go back for it—assuming I have the funds to pay for it directly.

For larger purchases, such as a car, a new roof, or a vacation, realize that if you can't afford to pay for it now, you won't be able to afford to pay for it later. Let's take a new car, for example. If you can't save $400 a month for a year for a $4,800 down payment, what makes you think you'll be able to afford a $400 car payment? People tell themselves that they'll make it work but in most cases, it does not. If you have a car that works and simply want to buy a new one before something happens to yours, start saving now. My rule is to save 50% for any large purchase. Better yet, pay cash. At minimum, have a payment that is no more than $300 a month. I realize you may not be at this point yet but as you begin to experience abundance and grow your income, I want to ensure you have set up rules and standards to live by.

Pull your credit report. When was the last time you checked your credit report? The interest you pay for items such as your mortgage, car, or even your car insurance, is all based on your credit score. If you have great credit, congratulations! No matter what past or financial hardships you have had, you must begin the process of cleaning up your credit. Before Dave and I got married, we had a lot of debt. I had student loans and lots of business debt. Dave's credit cards were pretty much all maxed out. We went for consumer credit counseling and the counselor worked with all of our creditors to reduce our interest rate and set up payments that went right to the principal balance. It took four years to be debt-free. I can still feel the joy of that moment today, 20 years later. I never want to be in that kind of debt again. If you are buried under debt, and are not sure where to start, visit my website at www.GYGB.com and click through our resources. We have vetted companies that are ethical and that will help you get your debt under control (including mortgages). You can also find access to free credit reports.

Eliminate waste. We are spoiled. While you may not think so, in general, if you have a roof over your head, food to eat and the discretionary funds to purchase this book, you are already ahead of 95% of the world's income earners. No matter how bad you think you have it, someone has it worse. If you are committed to financial control and peace of mind, it's time to consider the financial waste in your life and dump it. You may be thinking, "What is she talking about? I am frugal and don't have a penny to spare at the end of each month." But some of what you consider must-haves in reality are perks you could temporarily go without as you work to break the handcuffs of financial bondage. Circle the expenses below that you could eliminate (even if it would be painful) and underline those that you deem essentials. As you complete this exercise, remember that I am only asking you to ponder giving them up for six months to a year so that you can apply those extra funds to paying off debts, building a savings and getting in control of your finances:

» Cable (can run from $75-$300 a month)

» Cell phone or cell phones for children

» Eating out or take-out

» Coffee at your favorite coffee shop

» A car for every driver in the house

» Air conditioning set low or heat set high

» Newspaper and magazine subscriptions

» Gym membership

THINK LIKE THIS GIRL

If you can't manage $50,000 a year, you won't be able to manage $500,000 a year. Learn to manage the money you have and you will be blessed with more.

Of the items you circled, how much could you save? Where would you put this money? When can you start?

Have a giving heart. The more you *give,* the more blessed you will *be.* This law is very real. Learning it can be scary and takes a leap of faith, but once you've experienced it, you won't doubt that a generous spirit opens you up to receive more. You've just got to have the courage to take a leap of faith. When giving from the heart, you do not expect anything in return. The first time you do this it will be difficult, yet the joy you will feel after you write that check is indescribable. Knowing that you made an impact on someone's life or an organization in need is unlike anything else. In time, you will see those gifts returned tenfold. While you may not have a lot to give, I challenge you to give what you can. Consider putting your gift on auto pay, as if it were a bill. Do this and you'll avoid the temptation not to give in a particular month. Pick an organization of your choice. The amount—$10, $100, or $1000—doesn't matter. Every dime counts.

Embrace the future as *yours*. I was once talking with a client who told me a frightening story. My client was sitting with a banker in New York City whose office had an amazing view of the city. The banker said, "Look out the window and see everything below us—the buildings, houses, cars, businesses. We own it all, everything." This story gave me chills because it is so true. Banks hold the mortgages to our homes, the loans on our cars and the credit lines for our businesses. My dream is that people will learn to enslave their money rather than be enslaved by it. I want people to be served by money instead of serving it.

Every day I speak with women who are burdened by debt. They work 40 to 60 hours a week, receive their paychecks, and then turn around and give it all to banks and creditors. It's a vicious cycle: work, pay, work, pay, work, pay. Year after year with no end in sight, people work just to pay others. Imagine a life where things are different! You put in 40 hours a week, not 60. Your money is deposited into your three accounts: expenses, spending and savings. You spend only on what you really need to live. Bills are paid on time. You don't owe anything to bankers other than perhaps the interest on your home or car. You are debt-free and have the money you used to spend on interest to credit cards to pay for things such as family vacations, a new bike, or a pretty new item for the house. You work to pay yourself, not others. You may not live in luxury, but you live a life of financial confidence and peace of mind. You lay your head down at night knowing that your financial job has been well done. This is the future I want for you.

THE POWER OF GRATITUDE

As you begin to make peace with your finances, have true gratitude. Manage money well, and open yourself up for financial abundance, and money will start to flow to you. There is no limit. But know this: Anyone who has money has worked for it. There are no shortcuts. Money has to be earned and there are very specific life rules each of us must follow.

It's your turn to create your own path. It's your time to define the role money has in your life and how you will use it. As a woman, you must master this message and pass it on to those you care about. You have the ability to transform someone else's life by first transforming your own.

MANAGE LIKE THIS GIRL:
Chapter Summary

1. Repeat this affirmation daily: "I am my own lottery ticket!"

2. To attract money into your life, you must first understand what it means to you and the impact it has on your life. You need a healthy relationship with money in order to attract it.

3. You will never attract more money if you are not first grateful for what you have right now. To acquire more, you must have an attitude of gratitude and respect money by managing it appropriately.

4. You will never attract more money if you don't first learn to manage what you have.

5. Set up three bank accounts and begin distributing your money into them for a financial system that brings control over your finances: expense, spending, and savings accounts. Have your paycheck and any other income auto-deposited into these three accounts.

6. Enroll in online bill pay. This will eliminate waste on late fees and reduce the temptation to spend what you don't have.

7. If you can't afford to pay cash for something, don't buy it. Cut up all your credit cards except for one, which is only for travel and true emergencies.

MANAGE LIKE THIS GIRL:

Chapter Summary

(Continued)

8. Pull your credit report and educate yourself on repairing it if need be. A strong credit report is within your reach. While it may take time to clean it up, once it's rebuilt an entire new world will be open to you.

9. Make giving a priority. Generosity is an essential part of financial freedom. We who are blessed must pass on those blessings to others.

chapter ten

BREATHE

LET'S TALK REAL WORLD

Not a week goes by that I don't find a way to impart to my daughter, Paris, how fortunate she is to have been born at this time in history, in the United States. It is so important to me that she grasp the significance of this gift. She has opportunities that others will never get and she must honor both the women who are repressed in the world and those women before her who fought and paid the price that allows her to live the life she has today.

As women, we must understand our history. In my own family, my grandmother, Lela Keeler, had a third grade education. Women of her generation were denied the right to vote. Their voice was insignificant and their only career options were to be secretaries or nurses. A woman could not get a credit card unless her husband went to the bank and signed a note on her behalf. Want to own a house? Get a husband and then and only then could that dream come true.

My mother graduated high school and married at 18. By the time she was 24 she had three children and by 26 she was divorced, with no skills for navigating life on her own. Yet because of the women before her, who fought and opened doors, my mom had a voice. She could vote, she could work in a variety of jobs, and she could get a loan on her own. Still, the pay discrepancy between men and women performing the same job was huge. While my mom could put out twice the work, she received half the pay.

I was the first woman in my family to graduate from college. I was not married until I was 28, and didn't have my first child until I was 32. I had the opportunity to pursue any career I wanted and the pay gap between men and women, for the most part, had been bridged. I bought a car on my own, a house, and have voted in every election. My voice has been heard and, now more than ever, it counts.

How *This* Girl Does It: *Julie Podewitz*

My mom wakes up every day and asks, "Who can I positively affect today?" That's what I try to do. What I love about my job is giving others what they need and want. I have a bell that I ring when one of my clients achieves something. I get so excited when this happens! That's when I feel like I have my girl. Seeing other people reach their goals is what it's all about. My best piece of advice is to be a giver. And you know what? The best time to give is when you think you can't. Abundance comes when we give back.

Women have become a force to be reckoned with. For the first time in history, women are at the helm of Fortune 500 companies and are starting businesses at a record pace. We have earned this right and our firm place in history, yet our work is not done.

As you and I and our American sisters travel this journey together, it's our responsibility to continue to be the voice of change for women all over the world. Women are still being tortured, repressed and burdened. Rather than look away from their painful, grinding circumstances, we must turn to these women and raise our voices, open our wallets and help them experience the transformation we have seen here in the United States. While you may not think your voice or ten dollars will count, it does. Every effort makes a difference. Remember, what you do with your life teaches your daughters, nieces, sisters and girlfriends. A statement you make could change the course of a young girl's life and through your words, she could become an agent of change.

Take the time to look around, listen, and become aware of your environment. We tend to take so much for granted. When you are talking to your girlfriends about how stressed you are, consider the mother in the Congo who has just been raped for the third time by a bunch of thugs who are hell-bent on taking her last shred of dignity. Or think of the young girl of 12, living in Yemen, who is married off to a man twice her age. Rather than shut your eyes, open them. You will grasp the power of this book in a way you never dreamed possible. Knowledge is power. As a woman, you have the ability to use that power to effect change, not just here but all over the world. One day, the Congo may be free of war and women may know peace, and children in places like Yemen will know what it's like to experience adolescence as a child should. In the meantime, we must not squander our opportunities to live full lives, of our own choosing, made possible by the women before us.

How *This* Girl Does It: *Cary Sherk*

As a teen I was super sensitive and when I heard of a need, I'd pick up the phone and call someone, or write a note to the person in trouble. Now as an adult, in gratitude for getting my girl back, I just launched "Deborah's Notes," a formal card ministry for women and children. We have 29 women and children who are willing and able to write those notes of encouragement. Because my older sister died when I was little, I was so lost. I never really felt like I had my girl. But now, I feel like I'm getting her back again, and I plan on helping others do the same.

How *This* Girl Does It: *Michele Hockwalt*

My four friends in college constantly encouraged me. They saw something in me that I didn't see. They supported me, and they helped me understand how to have more confidence.

Life happened. With careers and kids, we lost touch through the years. As I was finding my girl again, I realized how much I missed that connection. I decided to reach out and reconnect with them, and now on the first Saturday of every month, our families, kids included, get together. If something comes up (work, etc.) that means a friend can't make it, we all adjust our schedules and make it work.

We make a plan. We keep a theme. We all chip in for food, and even a signature cocktail! Last month was Nerd night, the month before, Mardi Gras. We spend the night, taking turns at each other's houses. We set it up for success, by taking away all of the reasons why "we can't go," and we enjoy one another's company. It has been of one of the best things that I've done and has improved my life tremendously.

I challenge you to transform your vocabulary and to choose your words carefully going forward. Rather than saying how stressed, overwhelmed, or exhausted you are, think for a moment instead of the women in Dafur or Afghanistan who really are stressed, overwhelmed and exhausted. They don't have a choice in their situations but you do. If you feel stressed all the time, change your situation. What is making you stressed and what can you do about it, starting today? More than ever before, you have the power, resources, tools and support to change who you are, what you do, and the very life you live. If you have a daughter, no matter how old she is, it is your responsibility to teach her to use her own power and to understand the opportunities in front of her.

Imagine for a moment that you were born in another place and time. Imagine how different life might have been if you were born in India. Rather than a beautiful three bedroom house with two full baths and a yard to play in, your family might live in a cardboard box on a crowded street, scavenging trash cans for scraps of food that do little more than sustain life. If you were born in China, there's a good chance you would have been smothered at birth and if given the opportunity to live, you would have lived a life of silence and submission.

While you might not like to think of such things, doing so will force perspective. To receive abundance, you must first be grateful for what you already have. It is my hope that you'll look at your life through a different lens, and begin to give thanks for the blessings in your life. Make it a point to single out the little things that you currently take for granted: the bed you sleep in, a warm shower to bathe in, the toothbrush to cleanse your teeth. While this is and always has been a given in your life, for others it's nothing more than a dream. While you may hate your car, consider the person who commutes four hours a day on a complex bus system just to get to work. Suddenly your car doesn't seem so bad.

Getting your girl back is about finding your power. But to gain and keep your power, you must first understand the blessings in your

How *This* Girl Does It: *Shamim Wu*

I love to bring really talented women into my company. I've always hired people who are "green." I always wanted to do the same thing for people that was done for me. I was always given a shot at companies I started with, knowing that if I proved myself, I would succeed. I continue with that mantra today, in paying it forward. I'd rather work with someone who is eager and coachable than someone who thinks she knows it all. For women in leadership positions, it's important to always remember to give women a break the same way. I always remember to value the women I work with. Success breeds success!

life right now and build upon them. As you grow, it is important that you remove all self-imposed limits. As you get your girl back, you will understand once and for all that you are on a journey of constant growth, change and evolution. There is no destination but a continuous journey filled with possibility, accomplishment, failure, triumph and every emotion you will experience that is proof you are alive. We were put here to live. So, Girlfriend, go live your life in an amazing way. Leave a footprint on the world that no one else can fill.

When the time comes for you to take your last breath, inhale knowing you lived a life of purpose, opened every gift you had, and shared it with the world. Because of your willingness to identify and use those gifts, you changed the world. Know that you made the world a better place. In doing so you left a legacy others will strive to emulate. Those who loved you will find peace in knowing that you lived life on your own terms and were truly happy. My dear friend Delatorro McNeal wrote a book called *Robbing the Grave of Its Greatness.*[2] In this book Del describes the cemetery as the richest place in the world. He describes people who have gone to their graves with screenplays they wanted to write but never did, great books half-written, inventions never pursued, all because of fear. Such greatness could have been shared with the world but instead went to the grave. Don't let this happen to you. Die broke, give the world everything you have and do it with a vengeance.

My friend, it's been an incredible journey. Don't let the conversations end here. Join me on my blog at www.GYGB.com and Facebook (Get Your Girl Back Movement) to share your victories, experiences, failures and dreams and to let us support you as you enter the most amazing phase of your life yet.

2 Delatorro L. McNeal, Robbing the Grave of Its Greatness: 8 Steps to Birthing Your Best...Right Now (Tampa, FL: A Noval Idea, 2003).

> *Twenty years from now you will be more disappointed by the things that you didn't do than by the ones you did do. So throw off the bowlines. Sail away from the safe harbor. Catch the trade winds in your sails. Explore. Dream. Discover.*
>
> *—Mark Twain*

Tribe Pledge

I vow to support other women, even those I don't know.

I will offer them words of encouragement and kindness whenever possible, because God knows we need it!

I will never judge another woman, because I have not walked in her shoes.

I will resist all temptation to gossip.

I will lift other women up, helping to glue them back together when life tears them apart.

Join our Tribe, Won't You?

Traci Bild